INSIDE STORY

Printed and Published in Great Britain by D. C. THOMSON & CO., LTD., 185 Fleet Street, London EC4A 2HS.
© D. C. THOMSON & CO., LTD., 1988. While every reasonable care will be taken, neither D. C. Thomson & Co., Ltd., nor its agents accept liability for loss or damage to colour transparencies or any other material submitted to this publication.
ISBN 0-85116-418-8

£3.10

WHAT THIS SEASON HAS IN STORE . . .

SPRING FEVER!

SPRING CLEAN!

Freshen up your skin and stick to a strict skin care routine . . .

CLEANSE your skin every morning and night with an appropriate cleanser for your particular skin type. If you have dry skin then, generally speaking, a cream or thick liquid cleanser works best. For oily skin choose a milk or lotion cleanser.

TONE your skin to freshen it up, remove any traces of dirt or cleanser and help close up the pores. Alternatively, use a fine mineral water spray.

MOISTURISE your skin to keep it soft and supple. Choose a light moisturiser for day-time and a slightly heavier one for night-time. Pay special attention to dry areas such as your cheeks.

SEALED WITH A KISS

Get set for Valentine's Day with the perfect pout . . .

1. Outline your lips with a lip pencil, resting your little finger on your chin to steady your hand.

2. Coat a lip brush with colour from your lipstick and carefully paint the colour on to your lips, keeping within the outine.

3. Blot your lipstick on a tissue then apply another coat and blot again.

FOOLED YOU!

April Fool's Day is famous for silly jokes and pranks but what happens when you're faced with a real disaster which you don't find very funny . . .?

You've tackled a home dye kit and your hair has turned a natty shade of BLUE! First of all, don't panic and reach for the brown paper bag. Nor should you rush out and buy yet another kit to transform your hair to 'mousey brown'. Instead, admit defeat, go to your hairdresser for advice and hopefully they'll be able to sort things out.

In future, if you want to tackle a home dye kit follow these tips . . .

1. Always read the instructions carefully and do a skin test if one is recommended.

2. Get a friend to help — you'll get a more even result if there's someone else to reach the tricky bits.

3. Never colour your hair if you've just had a perm — wait at least a few weeks.

4. Never bleach your hair — that should be left to the experts.

5. If you're not sure of the shade you'd like then experiment with a wash-in, wash-out hair colour first.

BEAUTY WITHOUT CRUELTY

Look after all those Easter bunnies and resolve to use only cruelty-free beauty products. Try making a few yourself using natural ingredients.

Egg Shampoo

Separate the yolk from the white of an egg and beat each separately. Stir gently together. Massage through dry hair and leave for five minutes. Rinse off with tepid water — not hot or you'll end up with scrambled eggs!

Oatmeal Facial Scrub

Mix together 1 tablespoon each of finely ground oatmeal, orange peel and almonds into a paste. Place a teaspoonful on palm of hand and rub gently over face like soap. Rinse off.

Skin Freshener

Mash one ripe pear, sieve it and then apply to your skin. Leave for a few minutes then rinse off.

LOVE IS IN THE AIR

Make Valentine's Day extra-special with a message of love . . .

S.W.A.L.K. — Sealed with a loving kiss

I.T.A.L.Y. — I'll truly always love you

H.O.L.L.A.N.D. — Hope our love lasts and never dies

I HATE SCHOOL

A plain school skirt can come in v. useful. Wear it under a mini dress and pull on a pair of snazzy socks or tights to brighten things up. Sling your school satchel over your shoulder and don't forget those 'sensible' school shoes — v. trendy!

SCHOOL'S OUT!

School uniforms don't have to be confined to the classroom. Jazz up yours and leave the schoolgirl image behind . . .

A school blazer is ideal — it looks smart with a skirt or casual with jeans. A plain white school blouse also comes in handy, but make sure it *is* white and not a grubby grey. Don't limit your kit bag to just sports stuff — bung everything in it and use it after school too.

SCHOOL'S OUT!

If your uniform is quite distinctive then make the most of anything that's a bit different. Match up colours with the rest of your outfit, as we've done with this stripey blazer. Don't scoff at pigtails either — they're nice for a change and ideal if you haven't had time to wash your hair!

Skule No More!

The esteemed Ed lets you in on some memories from her schooldays (yes, she does remember that far back!)

I WISHED! I wished every day was my last, and failing that I wished for the 4 o'clock bell that dringed out freedom!

If you were like me, you wished you never had to go to school in the first place. I didn't only cry all the way to the school on my first day like all my other little pals, I cried all the way to school every day for a month! Then when I got to school I snuffled a bit more as my mum disappeared into the distance. Despite her turning round every five steps and waving frantically, I still believed I'd never see her again. She'd take her chance to be rid of this little cry-baby and scarper while I was at rotten old school!

Rotten old school! I didn't want to add up numbers *and then* take them away again! Pretty pointless really! I had other things to do — it was dolly's wash day, after all, and who would pour the invisible tea and pass the choccy bics at the Teddys' tea-party in the afternoon? No, as far as I was concerned school just got in the way of far more important things.

School did teach me some things, like how to reed and rite and that cats always sit on mats. And at least all my friends from my street were in my class. I'm surprised anybody could tell us apart, dressed as we were in indentikit grey duffle coats, white knee socks and satchels!

But why were boys so childish? They were totally useless back then unless you counted pulling your pigtails, kicking footballs at you or chasing you round the playground as useful! Boys always pushed to the front of the tuck shop queue. It was no good asking my big brother to help, he was the one pushing me out of the way! But don't worry, I got my own back on him later!

That was primary school of course. But soon the time came to say goodbye to all my plasticine models and things made out of drinking straws, because it was time to go to the big school!

The first thing I noticed about the big school was that it was big (and that it was also a school, unfortunately!) and I was little! It was a nasty shock changing school because I was no longer one of the "big ones" — I was back to being a "little one" again!

Suddenly everything was serious — sit up straight! No slacking! Stop lounging in the corridor, girl! That excuse just isn't good enough! Stay in after school! No, you're not excused PE! I don't care if your mother does come up to the school!

It was a blur of new things!

French? Er — isn't that what they speak in France, sir? Modern Studies! But it wasn't *modern* — it was everything that happened since 1900! Did they just do these things to puzzle you? And another puzzle was room no. 72. I don't think I ever found it!

You know what subject I hated most? Gym! It wasn't the running, jumping or getting really tired I disliked, it was those horrible blue uniforms!

Boys were marginally less hateful now — especially that dreamy one in 4B with the moody eyes and the latest LPs under his arm. The ones in my class put me in a mood and didn't have any records, they didn't even have a pen or pencil! How many times I got one returned after Geography chewed to death by a rogue pack of rabid beavers I don't know.

I remember getting my own back on my brother. It was so easy I almost felt sorry for him as he hopped about pleading with me to help with his homework because he had the most mega-important football match ever in the world ever to play. Pitiful!

Time passed and suddenly the dreamy moody boys were in the same class as me. Funny, some of them almost looked familiar, almost looked like those pimply spotty wretches who gnawed pens into an early grave. And since I wasn't allergic to wolf whistles, walking home wasn't such a bore any more.

Exams?? Aargh! Groan! Endless nights in talking on the phone to my very best friend about how I must start on my Maths revision right now but what about that Darren in the Chemistry class . . .

'Course I sailed through my final exams. No, I'm not showing you my grades! They were very good I'll have you know! Sniff!

Still, why should I care? Rotten old school, that's what I say! Mind you, lunchtimes *were* a laugh and English wasn't *too* bad, after all, Mr Rendall always was one of my favourites . . .

Maybe I'll walk by the rotten old school this afternoon, *but* I won't let anyone see me. Wonder if they'd remember me anyway — after all I did leave three weeks ago . . .

THE
GREAT
POP & TV & FILM
TRIVIA
Quiz!

OK, here's your starter for 10, fingers on the buzzers and throw a 6! It's the Great Jackie Pop & TV & Film Trivia Quiz, if you can get through this, you can go for your 5th Gold Run!

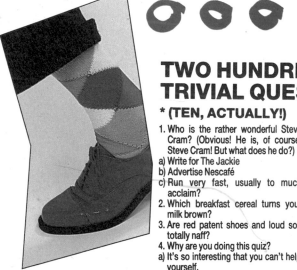

DOUBLE TROUBLE!

Well, Shepsie & Pirlie — they're a famous duo! Or should that be Pepsi & Shirlie? Anyway, see if you can correctly "pick a pair" from this list of slightly "jumbled" duos. (It will be highly rewarding if you do!) Ahem!

Phillip Schofield & Chris Lowe

Tom & Gnasher

French & Robin

Kim & Jerry (Might not be a bad idea)

Sue & Saunders

Batman & Gordon the Gopher

Dennis The Menace & Sooty

Neil Tennant and Mel

TWO HUNDRED * TOTALLY TRIVIAL QUESTIONS!
* (TEN, ACTUALLY!)

1. Who is the rather wonderful Steve Cram? (Obvious! He is, of course, Steve Cram! But what does he do?)
   a) Write for The Jackie
   b) Advertise Nescafé
   c) Run very fast, usually to much acclaim?
2. Which breakfast cereal turns your milk brown?
3. Are red patent shoes and loud sox totally naff?
4. Why are you doing this quiz?
   a) It's so interesting that you can't help yourself.
   b) There is nothing better to do since you've read the rest of the annual!
   c) You know all the answers!
5. Is George Michael nice looking?
6. How does the man who drives the snow plough get to work in the morning?
7. What is a gondola?
   a) An Italian sausage?
   b) A sub-machine gun?
   c) A boat you eat Cornettos in?

8. Who was Roobarb's arch enemy?
9. What was Spiderman's real name?
   a) Clark Kent
   b) Postman Pat
   c) Peter Parker.
10. Who skipped gaily about the mountains with Goat Peter?

10

GOLDEN OLDIES

OK, section 1 is a history lesson! But don't worry, nothing to do with wars! Read on and see how much you remember!

1. Who shot a POISON ARROW, then heard SMOKEY sing?
   a) Robin Hood
   b) ABC
   c) William Tell (he of the famous overture)

2. These lads lived in SUBURBIA with some WEST END GIRLS and now they'll never have to worry about paying the RENT. Who are they?

3. Which TV ad featuring a lad clad in boxer shorts, inspired the re-release of I HEARD IT THROUGH THE GRAPEVINE? (Clue: it wasn't Nescafé!)

4. Marti's mob's wish came true and they became very lucky, but do you know where they hail from?
   a) Darkest Peru
   b) Toytown
   c) Glasgow

5. Do you remember Duran Duran? (What do you mean, No!) They had a bit of a tiff and formed two mini-groups. Can you remember what they were called?

6. Who had a hit way back with the "ever popular" SUMMER HOLIDAY? (Ask your mum!)

7. THIS CHARMING MAN has a thorn in his side, but do you know Morrissey's full name? Is it:
   a) Stephen Patrick Morrissey
   b) Gareth Hunt Morrissey
   c) James Albert Spencer Morrissey.

8. Your mum jived to Lulu's shouting in the '60's, but can you spell Lulu's name? (Bit easy this one!!!)

9. Who were John, Paul, George and Ringo (not the crisps) better known as?
   a) Five Star
   b) The Drifters
   c) The Beatles.

10. Sinitta's Toy Boy had a Big Red One and Prince had a Little Red One! What on earth was it?
    a) Tomato
    b) A type of car
    c) A nose.

Wonderfully Interesting WORDSEARCH!

Can you unscramble the groups listed below in this utterly brilliant wordsearch? (Oh good, 'cos we can't!)

```
A B C S H B O N J O V I
T H A E E R A S U R E X
A L A R M U S H T A C G
S R L E M A H W M U O T
T I X U A P T A L S M E
N D S E L T R T H I M W
Q U E E N A H W L O U T
A O J K N I E M M W N E
R R I A C E H D E O A W
S N N K V A G Q A P R T
C A M E O K L N G L D E
B E A S T I E B O Y S W
```

AHA   ERASURE   OMD   BON JOVI
ABC   SLADE   HEART   COMMUNARDS
BERLIN   QUEEN   CULT   WET WET WET
WHAM   BLACK   ALARM   BEASTIE BOYS
CAMEO   T'PAU   GENESIS   BANANARAMA

CONTINUED OVERLEAF   11

THE GREAT
POP & TV & FILM
TRIVIA Quiz!

"WE 'NOSE' YOU KNOW!"

Would you know a rather famous person just by having a glance at their hooter? See how well you fare with these noses!

① ② ③ ④ ⑤ ⑥ ⑦ ⑧ ⑨ ⑩

CONTINUED ON P65

12

I GLANCED at my watch for the tenth time in as many minutes and saw, with a sigh of relief, that it was only five minutes until hometime. Double maths, last thing on Monday, was about as welcome as a boxed set of Richard Clayderman albums for Christmas.

Looking at the date at the top of the page surprised me. Monday 3rd October, 1988. I'd been at my new school for four and a half weeks and in the area for about two months. It felt like a lifetime. Don't get me wrong, I'm not complaining. Everyone was perfectly nice and I'd already made good friends with Sarah, but somehow I still felt very much like the new girl.

The more geriatric teachers still tended to lean closer and say to me, "Do you understand, dear?"

Suddenly, the bell clanged, bringing the lesson, and the day, to a close. A buzz of conversation spread around the room, "That wasn't an excuse to start chattering, children!" said Mrs Dicks, sourly. Children! What a woman.

"Collect the books in, Julie."

Without speaking, Mrs Dicks' favourite pupil rose and walked between the rows.

"Did you understand the work, Catherine?" Her eyes were fixed firmly on me.

"Sorry?" I said, surprised.

"Did you understand the work? It was a different examining board in . . . er, er . . . wherever you used to live. Different text books. Did you understand, dear?"

"Yes, Mrs Dicks!"

I saw Sarah was waiting for me at the main gates of the school, as I made my way down the pathway that led to the glorious freedom outside. She was picking clay off her hands and flicking it on to the pavement.

"No need to ask what you've been up to!" I said, disturbing her. "Is my six foot pottery statue of Rob Lowe ready yet?"

"Better than that," she replied, as we started to walk towards the bus stop. "Guess who was talking about you all the way through the pottery lesson? Kenny!"

"Kenny?" I said, as casually as I could. Now there was the perfect example of how being new about the place could be a problem. Sarah and I were already good friends, and we'd found a couple of badminton partners — Kenny and Mike Walsh. I really liked Kenny, but still didn't feel confident enough to spill the beans to Sarah. Maybe it would foul things up and ruin a good friendship between the four of us.

"Yeah, Kenny," she said, with a smile. "He was going on about how athletic you were! I think he's definitely got a thing about you."

I suspected something myself along these lines. I'm not being big-headed, it's just the way I catch his eye sometimes.

"Why?" I asked. "What do you think of Kenny?"

"He's a very nice guy . . ." she replied. I felt my heart sinking. That would really make a mess of things, if Sarah had a thing about Kenny.

"Yeah, he's nice," she continued. "But not my type at all."

I felt a smile break out all over my face. Sarah laughed.

"Oh yes," she said. "I wonder what's making you so happy? Go on, tell all!"

"I do like Kenny," I said. "But . . ."

"You thought I liked him as well? No, not the way you mean. I've known him since I was five. He's like a . . ."

"Brother?" I suggested.

"No, a wart. Only kidding. Are you on for a game of badminton tonight?"

"Of course," I replied. We had a weekly, platonic date with Kenny and Mike for mixed doubles at the youth club — it was the highlight of my whole week . . .

What a wally I was

As usual, Sarah and Mike gave Kenny and I a severe hammering on the badminton court. As the shuttlecock bounced off my racquet and into the net, I cursed under my breath. What a wally I was at sporty stuff. It was a good job Kenny was even worse than me.

"Never mind," said Kenny, as we walked off the court. "It could be a rainy Monday night."

I caught myself before I said it was a rainy Monday night.

"Ha, ha, Kenneth," I said. "There's only one thing worse than being a smart Alec . . . and that's not being a smart Alec."

Then he did something that made me want to turn him round and put my arms around him. He smiled.

I melted — he was gorgeous. Dark, curly hair hung neatly down his neck and behind his ears, and when he smiled, his eyes did too . . .

I snapped out of it. There I was, walking beside him and staring up at him, open-mouthed. Stop making it so obvious, I thought.

"Shall we go for a Wimpy?" he said as we came to the separate doors of the girls and boys changing rooms.

"Yes," I replied immediately.

"Are you two coming?" he said, as Sarah and Mike came up behind him.

"All right," said Mike. Sarah nodded her head. "OK!"

For one brief, glorious

moment I had thought he was going to ask me for a date. Maybe Sarah had got the wrong end of the stick in her pottery class. Perhaps he didn't fancy me at all. Maybe he was just being polite or friendly. I didn't want to think like that though, to be honest. I hoped it was shyness that was holding him back.

The problem was, I never

P.S. I LOVE YOU

Specially written for Jackie by Mark Roberts

seemed to get a chance to be on my own with him. Chance would be a fine thing, but as a part of a group and as the new girl in town, I didn't want to push my luck.

Sarah slid down in her seat

Sarah took the straw out of her mouth and placed her strawberry shake on the table. "It's madness," she said. "We spend a whole hour on the court killing ourselves, sweating off at least five pounds, and then we come in here and put it all back on again!"

"But you're not fat, Sarah," said Kenny.

"No, you've just got big bones. Very big bones," laughed Mike.

"My brother's never heard 'This Charming Man' by The Smiths, but I've been told it's not about him," Kenny added, as Sarah slid down in her seat.

"You shouldn't have any problem on the skiing holiday though, Sarah."

"Go on, Mike. What's the punchline?" asked Sarah, sighing.

"Well, Hannibal managed to get an elephant over the Alps!"

The thought of the skiing holiday brought me down from cloud nine pretty quickly. It had all been arranged and paid for long before I moved into the area or to the school. To add to the depressing fact that my friends were all going away together was the thought that it was at half-term, the last week of October.

Half-term! Whoopee, a whole week to wash my hair, paint my nails and watch 'Rainbow' on the box.

"Are you OK?" Kenny's gentle voice lifted me out of my thoughts. "You look a million miles away."

"Oh yeah, yeah," I said, trying to be cheerful. "I was just thinking . . ."

"That explains the glow of electric light around her head," said Mike, in a schoolteacher's tone of voice. Then he turned

sideways, to talk to Sarah, and torment her instead.

"He's not a bad lad," said Kenny.

"When he's asleep," I added.

"He doesn't mean these things nastily."

"I know he doesn't, Kenny. Mike's a really good laugh," I sipped my Coke through the straw, and rattled the ice at the bottom of the carton. "There'll be plenty of ice on the skiing holiday," I said.

"Yes, but will we be able to drink our Coke with it?" smiled Kenny.

"Are you looking forward to going?" I asked.

"Yes . . . and no!"

"What?"

"I am looking forward to it, but it's a shame you can't come along, Cath."

I felt like giving him a kiss he'd never forget.

Instead I sat where I was and smiled at him.

"That's a nice thing to say."

"I'm a nice kind of guy," he answered.

"Send me a card while you're away," I said.

"Of course I will. They don't have rude ones over there, though, so it'll have to be a nice one."

"I don't think my mum would appreciate a dirty postcard, Kenny. What would our new neighbours think!"

"I'll tell you what," said Kenny, struck by a good idea. "When I get back, I'll take you to the Sparta Sports Club for a game of singles badminton."

"The Sparta! Isn't that the new posh one?"

"Yeah, it is a bit plush. Do you fancy it?"

Fancy it? Absolutely, positively, definitely and without a doubt.

"Erm . . . yes, that'd be great, Kenny."

"We'll get some practice in and beat these two cheats."

"Oh, here we go," groaned Mike. "The shuttlecock was out of shape, a breeze blew in and took it over the line, I couldn't find my 'Hi-Tec' trainers and so I couldn't get a decent footing

15

because they've just varnished the court. How many more excuses do we have to make for you two born-again losers?"

"Mike," said Kenny, calmly.

"Yes, brother!"

"Belt up, you wally."

"Oh . . . OK!"

"All right then, Cath," Kenny said, turning back to me. "After I come back from holiday, we'll go to the Sparta."

"You're on."

She seemed to amuse her friends

I didn't bother to go and see the coach off, as it left school on the Friday night. It was bad enough listening to everyone going on about the trip, and showing off all their gorgeous ski gear.

Lynn Pratt (which was a pretty good description of her personality, as well as being her name) seemed to know the price of her own and everyone else's clothes. I had sussed her out very early on in the term as being the class bozo, and the things she was saying did nothing to raise her standing in my eyes.

She seemed to amuse her friends though, as she ripped into what everyone else was taking on the trip.

"Have you seen what Jenny Collins is taking? I wouldn't be seen dead in it. Mind you — if I was Jenny Collins, I wouldn't be seen dead anyway." Ha ha ha.

The week passed slowly, very slowly. By Sunday night, I was sick to death of listening to my tapes. On Monday, I seriously considered storming the television studios and kidnapping Zippy, thus putting an end to 'Rainbow'. By Tuesday, my hair almost begged me not to be washed again. Wednesday was largely taken up with writing to my penpal in Austria. All seven attempts at a letter read like suicide notes and ended up in the wastepaper basket.

But it was after Wednesday that the week could only get better!

Or so I thought.

For on Thursday morning, I had hope. The hope of a postcard from Kenny. I worked it out. If he arrived in Italy on the Saturday, and sent a card off to me sharpish, then it could arrive any time after Wednesday.

I woke up early on Thursday morning, and listened for the sound of the postman's heels click-clacking up the path. The digital clock by my bedside blinked the time, 8.48, as Mike Smith waffled quietly over the airwaves. Then, the gate creaked and I heard him coming briskly up the path. The spring on the letterbox snapped back. Click-clack-click-clack into the distance.

I threw the sheets back and hurried to the top of the stairs. There, in the hallway, was a small pile of mail. As I ran down the stairs, Mum made her way into the hall.

"I'll get it," I cried.

"Oh!" she said, and stopped dead in her tracks.

I scooped the mail up in my eager hands and advanced towards the telephone stool. I sat down. The top letter was from the Inland Revenue for Dad. The next one was a gas bill for Mum and Dad. The next one was for the people who lived in the house before us. The one after that was an airmail letter from Australia for Mum. The last one was a circular from the bank to Mum.

My heart fell inside me like a heavy stone dropping down a deep well.

"Never mind, love," said Mum. "There might be a card in the afternoon post."

The afternoon post came, but still there was no word from Kenny. Just as there was no word the next morning or afternoon.

When the last delivery of the week arrived on the Saturday morning I went to my room and hung my head in my hands. He's probably too busy having a good time to be thinking about me, I thought sadly. It occurred to me that I'd let my imagination run away with me — perhaps there was nothing there between us in the first place. The idea alone brought a lump to my throat.

Outside, it was a brisk, autumnal day. The only thing I could think of to lighten my feeling of doom was to take the dog to the park and watch him pretending he was still a puppy in amongst the leaves.

As I was pulled along the street by my over-anxious mutt, a thought occurred to me that I

would never have thought possible on the Saturday before a return to school.

At least I'll be back at school on Monday!

"It was fantastic"

I called for Sarah, earlier than I normally did, on the Monday morning, and found her bleary-eyed at the kitchen table. "We didn't get back till eleven o'clock last night," she yawned. "Did you have a good time?" I asked, calmly. What I really wanted to do was say to her, "What did Kenny do? Where was my card?"

"It was fantastic," she said. "We had a really good laugh." Sarah, though I wasn't aware of it at that moment, was getting me ready for what I was about to go through at school that day. Well, some of what I was about to go through. If it had been bad the day they left on the skiing holiday, the day after they returned was awful.

I sat at my desk and got my books out, with a whirl of chit-chat spinning around my head. It seemed that everyone, without exception, had had a fantastic holiday.

"Brilliant . . . incredible . . . skiing . . . piste . . . gorgeous instructor . . . skis . . . disco . . . hilarious . . . broken leg."

Certain words seemed to leap out of the wall of sound in the classroom, until the noise of chatter turned into a hail of suggestive whistles.

I looked up from what I was doing and saw Lynn Pratt strolling into the room with her Joan Collins expression on her face. Look at me, everyone, I'm a woman of the world. I wondered who she'd been seen with, an Italian waiter or a Spanish pop star or both maybe?

Her cronies slowly but surely left their places and sidled over to her desk, where she quietly got her books out.

"Pardon?" she said, to some mumbled question. "I don't wish to discuss it, Marlene."

Oh God, I thought. So that's it. I'm a woman in love and love never needs to tell its secrets! Not until playtime, at least.

Then I heard something that made my skin virtually crawl off my bones. I heard, "Mumble mumble blah rhubarb mumble Kenny mumble!" Suddenly, I felt revolted and interested.

Slowly, I turned to speak to Jenny Collins, half-wittedly.

"Not bad. A bit busy but, you know. OK really. You?"

"It was dead good. I didn't break my leg or anything."

I didn't pursue this line of conversation. I wanted to know what had been going on.

"Any blossoming romances on the slopes?" I smiled, falsely.

"Oh yeah, a few."

"E.g.?"

"Pardon?" she said.

"For example?"

"I'm not sure really but I heard a few things. Bette Francis got off with a ski instructor. Mike Walsh disappeared one night — don't know where. And, oh yeah, that reminds me. Kenny Walsh. Well, would you credit it?!"

"Would I credit what, Jenny?"

"He's going out with Lynn Pratt now!"

Just like that. Jenny's words were the last ones I recalled hearing that morning. All the others just swirled in the air around me. How could he do it? How could Sarah not say anything, knowing the way I felt about him? I suppose, I thought, I'm just still the new girl in town. They've only known me for a little while anyway.

I couldn't face Kenny

At lunchtime, I decided to avoid school. I couldn't face Kenny and I didn't wish to speak to Sarah after what she'd hidden from me. I went down to the park and sat by the lake where I fed my sandwiches to the ducks.

I kept looking at my watch and wishing that the hands would stand still; at least then I wouldn't have to go back to school and face everyone.

I shuffled along the path that led to the main building and listened to the bell ringing inside, calling everyone to lessons. Come on, it sang, come and get some more useless information. Why don't they give lessons on keeping feelings under control, or how to not be attracted to the wrong people? Why didn't they teach how not to get hurt?

"Are you all right, Cath?" Miss Ellis had her hand on my shoulder. I'd had my head down and had nearly walked right into her. I raised my head.

"Cath, you're crying. Are you all right?"

"I've got a headache," I ied.

"Come on," she said, "I've got a free period now. I'll take you home in the car."

I was sitting watching the six o'clock news, and trying to make myself believe that there were a lot of people worse off in this world than me, when the doorbell rang. I didn't think to get up and answer it. In fact, I didn't take my eyes off the television until I heard the sound of the living room door open and Sarah's voice.

"Hello, Cath," she said.

"Oh, hi, Sarah!" I half urned and then looked back at he TV again. Sarah came urther in to the room and sat down in an armchair.

"Are you all right, Cath?" he asked. She sounded concerned.

"I've got a bad head. That's all."

"Yeah, Miss Ellis mentioned t to me. I've been looking all over for you, all day. Where ave you been?"

"Around."

"Hey, Cath . . . what's the matter? You can tell me, I'm our friend."

"Are you?"

"Of course I am. Look, if 've done something, will you ust tell me and give me the hance to defend myself."

I took a very deep breath.

"Why didn't you tell me about Kenny and Lynn Pratt?"

"Tell you what?"

"That Kenny got off with er on holiday and that they're going out together now. Why idn't you tell me?"

"I didn't tell you because it idn't happen!"

I let the words sink in before replied.

"It didn't happen?"

Sarah shook her head.

"But Jenny Collins said hat . . ."

"Jenny Collins was in bed y nine o'clock most nights. he's just repeating the gossip. OK — Lynn Pratt made it pretty bvious to Kenny that she was nore than interested in him. In act, I've never seen such a latant display of flirting in my fe, but he wasn't interested. He idn't go near anyone on oliday."

Suddenly, I felt a mixture of ure happiness and a sensation hat surely I was about to wake p and find myself back at quare one. I was also very nhappy to think I'd thought so adly of Sarah.

"I'm sorry, Sarah," I said.

"Don't worry, Cath. You should trust me more in future."

"I will — promise."

"Anyway," said Sarah, brightly, "enough of this doom and despondency. Are you coming for a game of badminton?"

I still felt a bit delicate

"Oh yes!" I said, remembering our regular Monday meeting with Kenny and Mike. I still felt a bit delicate and had been crying a lot.

"I look a bit of a mess," I said.

"You don't. Go and give yourself a quick wash. You'll be fine."

"I'm not being funny, Sarah, but I'd rather not. Not tonight. Make my apologies?"

"OK, Cath, no problem." Sarah stood up to leave. "I'll have to go," she said. "They'll be waiting."

"Oh, by the way!" She opened her bag and fished around inside it. "This arrived at our house for you today."

She handed me a postcard with an Alpine scene on the front of it. I turned it over. It was a card from Kenny, addressed to me, care of Sarah's house.

"I couldn't remember if you were 35 or 53. So I told him to send it to my house. Better late than never."

I waved to Sarah as she disappeared down the road, and hurried back inside the house. I read the words on the back of the card, gazed at his handwriting and was delighted to see three kisses after his name.

Perhaps I wasn't imagining things after all. Maybe he did miss me when he was away.

Better late than never

I went upstairs and turned my tape recorder on. I lay on my bed and looked at the picture on the card, and then at his writing. I slid it under the cool, crisp linen on my pillow and smiled. Better late than never.

As my mind wandered and thoughts turned to how nice he was to me when we played badminton, I hardly noticed the tape ending. Time, for a change, was flying.

The doorbell rang. Probably it was for Mum or Dad, couldn't be for me. Downstairs I heard the door opening and the sound of

voices in the hallway. The peaceful atmosphere of my room was suddenly disturbed by the sound of Mum's voice shouting up the stairs.

"Cath!"

I got off my bed and headed straight for the door.

"Cath, there's someone here to see you."

I walked to the top of the stairs and looked down. Standing in the hall was Kenny, smiling up at me and with a paper bag in his hand.

"I've brought something back for you from holiday."

I managed to restrain myself and walked down the stairs one at a time. I smiled.

"Hiya, Kenny. Have a nice time?"

"I missed you, but yes, it was a nice place."

He handed me the bag. I opened it up and saw that it was full of hand-made Swiss chocolates.

"Thanks for your card."

"Listen," he said, glancing at his watch. "I was thinking. If we hurry we'll catch the pictures. Unless — have you still got a headache?"

Funny — it seemed to have gone.

"I'll just go and get my coat," I said, as I turned and headed to the coat closet under the stairs. I took my coat down and smiled in the shadows.

"Kenny!" I said.

"Yes?"

"I missed you too."

WatER

Water can work wonders, so grab your rubber duck, sponges, lotions and potions and spoil yourself.

Bathtime isn't just for getting clean, it's also perfect for relaxing and can give you a real boost. You can use a bath to wind down, wake up or simply feel fresh all over.

Some Like It Hot

A warm bath will help to soothe tired muscles and relieve aches and pains, especially after strenuous exercises.

But don't have the water too hot or you might feel a bit light-headed. Also too many hot baths may damage and dry out the skin, so take care!

Cool Down

A cool bath is great for waking you up in the morning and making you feel fresh and bright.

It's also great if you've been out in the sun too long as it really does help soothe sunburned limbs. In fact make it as cold as you can possibly bear, because the colder it is the more effective it'll be in preventing sun from penetrating deeper layers of skin.

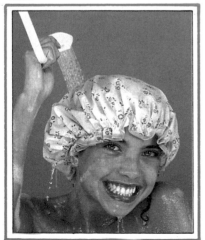

Spice It Up

First thing in the morning or when you're getting ready to go out, pep yourself up by adding bath oils. You'll find loads of these around and The Body Shop and The Body and Face Place do a great range at reasonable prices. Try tangerine, geranium, lemon and orange to help lift the spirits.

Calm Down

When you're feeling tense, depressed or whacked after a hard day, come home to a bath

containing Marjoram, Camomile or Juniper. These will calm you down and give an all over feeling of well-being!

Before

Before you get into your bath give your body a good rub with an exfoliating lotion or body brush to get rid of all those dead cells and leave your skin silky smooth.

Don't forget that moisturising bubble bath and bath oils will help too.

If you've got some patches of dry skin eg. heels, elbows, then rub some moisturising cream into these and then get into the bath and let the water do its stuff!

During

Once you're in the bath lie back and relax, or use the time to pamper yourself by giving your hair a deep conditioning treatment, or massage your feet and try a pumice stone on them to get rid of any nasty dry patches.

Don't be tempted to stay in the bath too long or top up cooling water with some nice hot stuff. About half an hour is the longest you should stay in, any longer and your skin will look like a dried prune!

After

After bathing, dry yourself briskly with a dry towel. Then apply lashings of body lotion all over.

Face packs are most effective after baths too, because the steam will have opened up your pores.

Water Sports

Surprisingly, you can get fit in the bath too as working against the force of the water is very effective.

Practise sit-ups, or lie back lift one leg, hold for a few seconds and put down then repeat with the other leg.

BABy

Hey, Good-Looking!

Think that being a model is all catwalks and designer clothes? Then think again! We'll take you through a model's typical day. You'll be surprised how 'unglamorous' it is!

Rising at the crack of dawn, rushing around modelling agencies with a portfolio tucked under your arm, having your hair and face pulled about for hours on end and then having to look wonderful for an impatient photographer — that's a model's almost daily routine! Not such a glam job after all, eh?

We'll take you through a day in the life of a model just to let you know exactly what it's like for young girls (and boys!) nowadays trying to make their name in the modelling game.

Our model Barbie takes us through her day. Before she does anything, Barbie rings the agency to find out what appointments she has for that day just in case there's been any changes to any of her plans.

Then it's probably the most difficult job of the day — finding the photographer's studio! Just as well Barbie's got her A-Z of London. There're many studios in London it's impossible to know them all.

There's a lot to be organised as our photo sho... Lighting has to be correct — and Barbie's mak... It'll need touched up again every so of... as the hot lights mean it starts to slide off!

20

...bie meets with the photographer (eventually!) and shows him portfolio. All models have to have a portfolio of photographs of themselves to show to photographers, magazines and gencies so that the potential client can see if the model's look is suitable for the job they have in mind.

Then the preparations begin for the actual shoot. Time to get the make-up plastered on and the hair put into place. Barbie is lucky today, the client has provided a professional make-up artist to do the job. Sometimes she has to do it herself so that means she has to know which make-up will suit which lights and the colours etc. Make-up for a special shot can take anything up to four and a half hours!

And the finished article! We're sure you'll agree it was well worth all the hard work.

...ce she's been through all that, she still has to have the photographs taken! Phew! Who said a model's life was easy?

It's pretty easy to judge a fella by the togs he sports. Here's a little guide to help you recognise whether the man of your dreams could turn out to be a nightmare!

MR UNBELIEVABLY HIDEOUS TIE

Yes, I'm sure we've all seen him at one time or another. He's usually a bank clerk or has some other office job. At night he will team the tie up with an equally stomach-churning suit and shoes (red patent ones perhaps?). He'll slick his hair back, or at least attempt to. No doubt he's got lots of pens and a diary in his suit pockets. Your mum would probably like him, so that's a reason in itself to avoid him. He'd probably take you out and spend all night talking about the Stock Market or something else completely boring!

VERDICT:
Run a mile. These guys are only good for avoiding and not much else.

MR RED PATENT SHOES and TERRIBLE SOCKS

Look out for this one girls! Wow! Disco fever gets its revenge! This is the type of guy that hangs around the edge of the dance floor all night. Occasionally, though, he'll get up and boogie. That's when it's time to make your getaway. This guy would make Rick Astley look like a good dancer (and that's not easy!). Just remember not to stand too close to the dance floor when he's about, otherwise your eyes will be dazzled when the disco lights hit those oh so shiny shoes! This guy probably shaves his legs and is never without a comb in his back pocket.

VERDICT:
Unless he's a millionaire's son, STAY CLEAR, SISTERS!!!

impressions

MR BLACK SHIRT and WHITE TIE

This guy probably thinks he's a cross between Al Pacino and Rob Lowe, when actually he's a cross between Des O'Connor and The Bee Gees. He'll strut into the disco, eyeing up every female in sight — and then he'll probably trip over a stool. He'll lounge back in his seat and try to look cool. Odds on he'll be wearing a stupid tie pin in the shape of a dagger or something. You can bet he'll be wearing trousers three times too small as well. He'll have a better wiggle than your big sister and probably takes twice as long to get ready when he's going out anywhere. This is the type of guy who has furry dice in the front of his car. Would you look at that hat! Are you surprised he doesn't want to let us see his face?

VERDICT:

If you want to spend a date with a guy who only talks about his ex-girlfriends and how fast he drives his car (or should we say his dad's car!), then go ahead. If you've got any sense, though, you'll stay in and watch your goldfish swimming round their tank rather than die of boredom with this fellow!

WHAT THIS SEASON HAS IN STORE...

HERE COMES SUMMER!

A TASTE OF SUMMER

Look your best in that itsy bitsy bikini by counting the calories and sticking to a healthy diet . . .

	Calories per 100g
Apples	36
Grapefruit, raw	11
Vanilla ice cream	196
Lettuce	11
Mars Bar	447
Milk, fresh	66
Milk, fresh, skimmed	35
Orange juice	38
Potato crisps	559
Salad cream	387
Strawberries, fresh	26
Sugar, white	394

NATURAL BEAUTY

Keep your make-up to the minimum and go for the bronzed look this summer!

Forget about heavy foundation and go bare-faced or use a tinted moisturiser instead. If you feel naked without mascara, use a waterproof brand or, better still, have your eyelashes dyed. It only costs a few pounds at a beautician's and lasts for four to six weeks. Alternatively, use a home dye kit and tackle it yourself!

For lips, stick to just a clear lip gloss or special lipscreen to protect and moisturise them.

READY, STEADY, GLOW!

Follow our tanning tips and become a bronzed beauty . . .

* Take your sunbathing gradually. It may be tempting to lie out all day in the sizzling sun but don't — you'll only frazzle!
* Always use a good sunscreen with a suitable factor for your skin type. Remember, the higher the factor number the greater the protection.
* Never fall asleep in the sun.
* If you want to go for a quick dip now and again make sure you use a waterproof brand of sunscreen so you don't have to re-apply it so often.
* Beware of cloudy days — the sun's rays can filter through so you can still burn.
* Don't wear perfume on the beach as the ultra-violet rays can react with it and cause staining.
* To help keep your tan always use a good after-sun and moisturise your skin well after sunbathing.

SNAP HAPPY!

Make sure your holiday snaps turn out well by following our tips on taking pics . . .

* Read the instruction booklet provided with your camera before you go on holiday and, if it's a new camera, have a trial run using one film at home first.

* Buy your film before you go — it's usually cheaper at home than abroad.

* Remember to fit new batteries.

* Carry your film and camera in your hand luggage if you're travelling by air. Occasionally airports require you to remove them as some X-ray equipment can damage films.

* If you're going on holiday with a pal try to take it in turns to take photos, otherwise you'll end up with doubles of everything!

* Take care when you're about to snap — watch out for trees or poles growing out of people's heads, passers-by about to walk into the picture, fingers over the lens or worse, the lens cap still on!

THE ESSENTIAL BEACH KIT

1. **A sturdy bag.**
2. **Sun-tan lotion, sun-block and lipscreen.**
3. **Something to read (Jackie, of course!).**
4. **Two towels — one to lie on and one to dry yourself with.**
5. **A pair of sunglasses.**
6. **Personal hi-fi and some tapes so you don't get bored.**
7. **A wide-brimmed hat or special gel to protect your hair.**
8. **Some money. Just enough for the odd Cornetto — leave your travellers' cheques etc in the hotel safety deposit box.**
9. **Something to wear on your feet — hot sand can be painful!**
10. **A baggy T-shirt so you can cover up when the going gets hot.**

THE *Beauty* BUSINESS

Do you know your blusher brush from your eyelash curlers? Follow our quiz and find out . . .

1. You've just applied some foundation and are looking a bit pasty-faced. To add a touch of colour do you . . .
a. furiously pinch your cheeks until they turn scarlet
b. apply a light dusting of translucent face powder then stroke on a little blusher
c. use a colour corrective moisturiser?

2. Lipstick never seems to last on you so how do you avoid leaving your mark everywhere you go?
a. Apply several thick coats of lippy and hope for the best.
b. Lash on lots of lip gloss over your lipstick.
c. Apply one coat of lipstick, blot your lips on a tissue, apply another coat, then blot again!

3. Eyelash curlers are . . .
a. odd-looking contraptions which when pressed against your eyelashes will give some curl
b. special mascaras
c. little pink curlers, made famous by Hilda Ogden?

4. When is the best time to apply a face mask?
a. If you want to frighten off a boy who's been pestering you.

b. To hide your spots.
c. Just after a bath when the pores of your skin are open.

5. If you wear contact lenses you should . . .
a. take them out before you apply make-up
b. put them in before you apply make-up
c. shake them all about and do the hokey-cokey before you apply make-up?

6. Placing slices of cucumber over closed eyelids will do what?
a. Refresh tired eyes.
b. Give your eyelids a nice greenish tinge.
c. Make you look like a complete idiot.

7. How often should you get your hair cut to ward off split ends?
a. Every six months.
b. Every six to eight weeks.
c. Only when you start walking into lamp-posts.

8. What are cuticles?
a. The area of skin around the base of each nail.
b. The white areas at the tip of each nail.
c. Special scissors for cutting nails.

9. If your lips are too full how can you disguise it?
a. Outline your lips with a lip pencil just outside the natural lipline.
b. Use v. bright or frosted lip colours.
c. Outline your lips with a lip pencil just inside the true lipline then fill in with a matt-finish lip colour.

10. What is combination skin?
a. Where one side of your face is dry and the other is greasy.
b. A mixture of dry and oily skin, where the area around the eyes, cheeks and neck is dry and the forehead, nose and chin are slightly oily.
c. Skin which has a combination of spots and freckles.

Answers

1. b. Don't overdo the blusher though or it'll look v. false. 2. c. Get blotting! 3. a. Not as painful as they sound! 4. a and c. Depends what you look like without the mask! 5. b. 6. a and c. 7. b. (or c in the case of The Steve!) 8. a. 9. c. 10. b. (or c in the case of The Steve!)

* Only joking Steve!

SPORTSTYLE

BEING SPORTY ISN'T ALL 'JOLLY HOCKEY STICKS' AND SWEATY RUGBY JERSEYS — SPORTSWEAR IS THE STYLISH LOOK FOR BEACH OR BACKYARD, AND WHO KNOWS, YOU MIGHT FIND TIME TO DO SOMETHING ENERGETIC IN YOUR NEW SPORTS TOGS!

27

OUT FOR A JOG!

Whether you're running for that bus, Rob Lowe or your weekly Jackie it's v. important to look the part! Track suit top: Adidas Running vest and shorts: Nike.

28

IN THE SWIM!

100 lengths at lunchtime or going for the best tan ever in the whole wide world you still need a well-slinky swim number! Swimming costume: Olympus Sports.

ANYONE FOR . . .

Show off your volleying skill or just be a smash hit in these trendy tennis togs!
Tennis polo top and pleated skirt: Fred Perry.

ON THE PISTE

Swish this way and that on the slopes or slide down to the local cafe for a cosy cup of hot choc. Ski-wear: Blacks Outdoor Wear.

All these sports are ace for getting you into super shape in their own way. But why not go sports-mad and try all four! Beginners read on for our starter for 10 tips on how to get your sport out of the armchair and off the ground!

TENNIS TIPS

Le tennis! Ah, most trendee of sports. Who can forget the strawberries and cream, the brilliant green courts, McEnroe's tantrums . . . And that's just sitting in front of the box for the entire Wimbledon fortnight.

But if you want to get out there crashing in aces and lobbing away with the best of them then it's a cinch. Take one racquet and several balls and pop down the nearest municipal courts. An hour's hire is dead cheap between two. Oh, and you do need two of you.

Tennis is one of the richest sports in the world and this is reflected in the prices of some of the gear. But you don't have to get an endorsed-graphite-every-one-a-winner racquet at £2,000,000! Dunlop, Slazenger and Wilson all make great bats, er racquets for a lot less, around £20-30 to be precise.

Tennis buffs who do want to go quite crazy and buy gear endorsed by their fave players have some choice. Racquets, sweaters, shoes, fridges, turnips . . . the list is endless!

Oh, and those players! Ivan Lendl, Stefan Edberg, Boris Becker, Anders Jarryd, Michel Pernfors . . . drool! Roll on Wimbers!

WET WET WET

Swimming is reckoned to be the sport that's best for all-over toning up of your body. In that case, what are you waiting for? Dive in!

Aha! You can't swim! Well, take the advice of those ancient Rolf Harris ads on TV and get down to your local baths and learn. All swimming baths have beginners classes you can attend and it really is worth getting all the strokes taught by an expert. Swimming is like riding a bike, once you learn you never fall off or in!

The beauty of swimming is you hardly need any gear. In fact, it's a big help to not wear too much when dipping! That's not to say you have to stick to costumes that went out with the Ark. Speedo and Arena have a tremendous selection of super streamlined ones.

SPLASH!

ON THE RUN

You don't have to be Steve Cram or Liz McColgan to enjoy life on the run, jogging really is the sport for everyone from kids to grannies. It's also one of the cheapest sports around — all you need are the shoes and you're away (like the wind!).

If you do decide jogging is the thing for you then it's quite important to get the correct shoes. Because it's a little known fact that while you're jogging along having a jolly time admiring the birdies and nice flowers you're putting your poor little feet under several hundred pounds of pressure. Frightening, eh? So do search out the right footwear. Nike and Reebok have the best selection at v. reasonable prices. And they also do lots of well-cool running gear.

Once you've got the shoes, what next? Well, it's no good dashing out and trying to break the world record for the mile — you probably won't reach the end of your street. Start slowly and gradually, jog for two minutes, walk for two minutes, jog for two minutes. Don't be too disappointed if you can't manage even this, everyone has to start somewhere — even Coe & Co! You'll be amazed how soon you'll be able to build up to a couple of five minute jogs a week and then 10 minutes . . . 15 minutes . . .

Jogging is more fun with your mates and a good way to let that hunky boy in your class see how trim your legs are. 'Course he *might* not be able to catch you!

See you in the next Olympics!

SNOW FUN!

Well, not strictly true, ski-ing is brill fun but you do need a few essential items. It's no joke stuck up a slope shivering and chattering away unable to enjoy yourself because you're freezing.

The basic bits of gear you need include a warm ski jacket. As well as being dead trendy just now they don't cost an arm and a leg and C&A always have a great selection. Try and get a matching pair of waterproof overtrousers as well unless you like having wet legs. A good pair of waterproof gloves are another essential because you'll be picking yourself up out of the snow quite a lot at first. For your head you need something nice and cosy. Buy a ski hat if you want but maybe now's the time to dig out that warm tammy Granny knitted you last Crimbo!

Ski-ing might look easy pimps when you see Martin Bell and Peter Müller zipping down the slopes but don't forget they've been training for years and were virtually brought up on a diet of snow. But don't worry, every ski centre has qualified instructors to watch your every move and make sure you don't get into bother. If you don't fancy starting on the wet stuff then search out one of the many dry ski slopes around for your snowless start.

Happy slaloming!

WHEN THE HEARTBREAK BEGINS

YOU can't live with 'em and you can't live without 'em! No, not white Toblerones, silly, B.O.Y.S. — Boys! Now, boys are pretty secretive chaps and it's certainly not easy to know what goes on in their tiny brains (if anything at all!). And unless you know everything about football it'll be hard to strike up a conversation and find out.

But don't worry, we set all the Jackie expert boy-watchers to work and they've compiled The Essential Jackie Guide To Everything You Ever Wanted To Know About Boys!

Firstly we'll take you through BOYS' worst habits. But be prepared because there's quite a lot!

WORST HABITS

Nose-picking (yick!) in public
Leching after other girls when they're out with you
Belching and breaking wind generally
Shouting whenever you argue
Sulking if they lose the argument
Watching anything that remotely resembles sport on the telly
Expecting you to kiss them after they've eaten a ton of garlic
Wolf-whistling at everything in a skirt
Picking fluff from their belly-buttons
Saying they'll phone and then they don't
Poking you in the shoulder when they want to dance

Phew! Well, space and taste prevents us from printing any more icky BOYS' habits.

Do they have any good habits? Well, yes they do but they take a bit of spotting.

Of course, boys could have impeccable habits and still have truly awful taste in togs. So, it's time to move on to dress sense and boys' lack of it. Here, in no particular order, are our pet hates . . .

WORST WEAR

Tucking their jumpers into their jeans
Red patent shoes
Wearing socks in their bed (pooh!)
Snorkel parkas with fur trim round the hood
Tartan-type jeans
The dreaded flares
Bermuda shorts
"Snake" belts
Jeans which are baggy round the bum and nowhere else
Red leather ties
Fingerless gloves
Footie scarfs tied round the wrist
Footie socks under jeans
Wraparound sunglasses
Black slip-on shoes and white terry towelling socks
Tank tops
"Flecky" suits
Lumberjack shirts

BOYS! BOYS!

GOOD HABITS

Nice to their mum
Nice to your mum
They're always there for you to jump on during scary movies
They love your mum's cooking (someone has to)
They lend you their records
They let you borrow their shirts
They always finish your left-overs in restaurants
They teach you the words to dirty football songs
They don't borrow your lipstick
They help with your metalwork homework (are you sure about this one?)

Worra list, eh? But don't despair, there are a lot of dapper chaps out there and you can easily spot them if you memorise our next guide . . .

STYLISH STUFF

Skimpy black swimming trunks
Boxer shorts
Faded 501's
Johnny Woss suits
Next shirts
Denim shirts
Battered leather jackets
Chinos
Doc Martens
Boys in cycling shorts. Mmmmm! Mmmmm! Mmmmm!
Their birthday suits! Fwoah!

CONTINUED ON PAGE 38

BOYS!

CONTINUED FROM PAGE 36

Well-mannered and dressed to the nines some boys may be but it sorta spoils things when they open their gobs and say the most gorm things like . . .

YOU WHAT?

That's woman's work!
How about it, darlin'?
Any chance of a cup of coffee? (Nudge, nudge, blee!)
You know, you're *quite* nice . . .
Do you want to "get off" with me?
Fwoah! Look at the legs on her!
Hi, lads . . . this is my bird . . .
Aw, girls are like that, though!
What's wrong?
Do you want to go to a football match on Saturday?
But I wasn't doing anything, honest!
Don't get your knickers in a knot!
See you around!

With that classic "goodbye" line we'll leave

Swoony Sayings all rolled into one. If not, there's plenty more chaps around like . . .

Men You'd Like To Share A Sunbed With

George Michael
Tom Cruise
Rob Lowe
Mike from Neighbours
Jason Patric
Andrew McCarthy

Still Good-looking After All These Years — Old Lifies

Paul Nicholas
Paul Newman
Tom Danson (Cheers)
Dirty Den
Jim Robinson (Neighbours)
Robert Redford

Blue-Eyed Boys

Neil Tennant
Matt Goss
Luke Goss
Morten Harket
Clark Datchler

BOYS!

the stupid things boys say and try to think of the occasional nice things they come out with . . .

AWWWWW!

Erm, these are for your birthday (blush)
You look really nice tonight
You're more important to me than footie (Gasp!)
We were made for each other
You haven't really got a big bottom
Mmm! That's nice perfume
You don't *need* to go on a diet

If you're v. lucky you may at this very moment have your arm around Mr Perfect Manners, Mr Stylish Clothes and Mr

Dangerous Boys To Watch Out For

Marti Pellow
Matt Dillon
Pat Cash
Richard Gere
Mickey Rourke

Some Ways To Twist Boys Round Your Little Finger

Having the last two tickets for the big match
Wearing a black leather mini skirt
Cooking them a big tea
Giving them your v. last Rolo
Buying the new Inxs/U2/ Simple Minds LP
Letting them wear *your* denim shirt

BOYS' BANDS

Def Leppard
Inxs
U2
Bananarama
Heart
Simple Minds
Big Country
Any Hip-Hop Music

DEFINITELY NOT BOYS' BANDS

Wet Wet Wet
Bros
Pet Shop Boys
Johnny Hates Jazz
Pepsi & Shirlie

The 5 Most Important Things In A Boy's Life

His football
His food
His mum
His record collection
His car

5 Famous Footie Boys

John Barnes
Paul Gascoigne
Tony Adams
Gary Lineker
Charlie Nicholas

BOYS! BOYS!

5 Naff Things Boys Always Own

Furry dice
Flared jeans
Tattered posters of Sam Fox
A one-eyed, one-armed teddy bear
Acoustic guitars with no strings which they can't play!

BOYS' FOOD

Big Macs 'n' fries
Yorkie Bars
Mars Bars
Curries
Fish 'n' chips
Enormous sarnies with entire fridges in them
Their mum's cooking, your mum's cooking, anybody's mum's cooking . . .
Anything else edible really.

BEST BOYS

If you're a boy-watcher (and let's face it, who isn't?) then we're sure you'll have recognised all the best boys in our piccies. But just in case, turn this book upside down to reveal all.

Tom Cruise
Ralph Macchio
Nick Berry
Richard Gere
Michael J. Fox
Emilio Estevez
Jon Cryer
Matt Dillon
ANSWERS

So there you have it. Get boy-hunting!

SARAH DYCE age 16
"I love Marc Almond's knees. Hairy knees can be so sexy — but it depends who they're on, of course! I shave my knees, but I still think they're horrible. My most ticklish part is the back of my knees."

LISA HAZELGREEVES age 17
"Danny La Rue has nice knees (blee!), though I personally like a good piece of hairy leg (that's more like it!) I shave mine about every three weeks, otherwise they get pretty prickly."

CAROL HEY age 16
"The best knees are on Riff Raff of The Rocky Horror Picture Show (mega-pervy film). I don't really like knees, but they're pretty essential. I shave my legs and knees when I can be bothered. I wear tights but the stubble usually pokes through. I like boys with hairy legs — they're sexy!"

ANITA SHEPHERD
"Lloyd Cole has wonderful knees, but I don't like them hairy. I shave my legs but not my knees. I can't face my knees but I rather like boys in cycling shorts."

KIM MAISE, PAULA INKSTER and LINDSEY HOPPER all age 13.
KIM — "Matt of Bros — he's got lovely knees, and so has Rick Astley. I like my knees because they bend and they're useful. I would like to kiss Matt Goss's knees!"

PAULA — "Rick Astley's knees, now they're definitely sexy. I like my knees too, I talk to them in the bath."

LINDSEY — "Rick Astley's knees are pretty brill. I think everyone should have a pair because they bend at the back. I never shave my knees because you could cut your kneecap off!" (Blee!)

JAMES COLE age 47(?)
"Her beside me has the nicest I ever seen! I'm a bit lazy, I just sha mine at the weekends. (Eh?) I quite girls with hairy legs but I think a knees are an eyesore and should be off."
('Her beside him' is Cherilyn Coke 15).

NICE AND KNEESY!

Knees, aah yes, those dimply, tickly, all together bumpy things. Do we love or bathe them? Do we even bother to shave them? And are we tickly behind them? (Oooer!)

We asked some of you to take down your trousers and lift up your skirts!! (To see your knees, of course!!!)

CHERYL WESTGATE, age 15, JOANNE GRADY age 15, and CLAIRE MULHALL age 16.

CHERYL — "I like Michael Brandon's knees. ("Dempsey", out of DEMPSEY & MAKEPEACE.) I think legs are important, and good ankles and knees too. I think mine are OK. We'd be a bit limp without them, wouldn't we?"

JOANNE — "I like Phillip Schofield's knees, but I don't usually look at knees — it's the eyes I go for! You can't see boys' knees because of their trousers anyway! Waxing legs and knees is the best way to get rid of hairs."

CLAIRE — "Rob Lowe and Mark Shaw — they're a bit of all right. I've got knees like a footballer's, I shave them all the time but sometimes I miss bits, which is annoying. I like boys' knees to be hairy."

Knees need lovin' too!!

JOHN ASTHON age 16
"Sinitta has nice knees, well, actually they're not very kneeish, her legs sort of just go up and down with no bumps in them. I don't like girls with hairy legs."

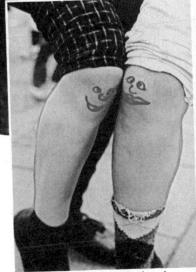

Knees are also quite useful for drawing on!

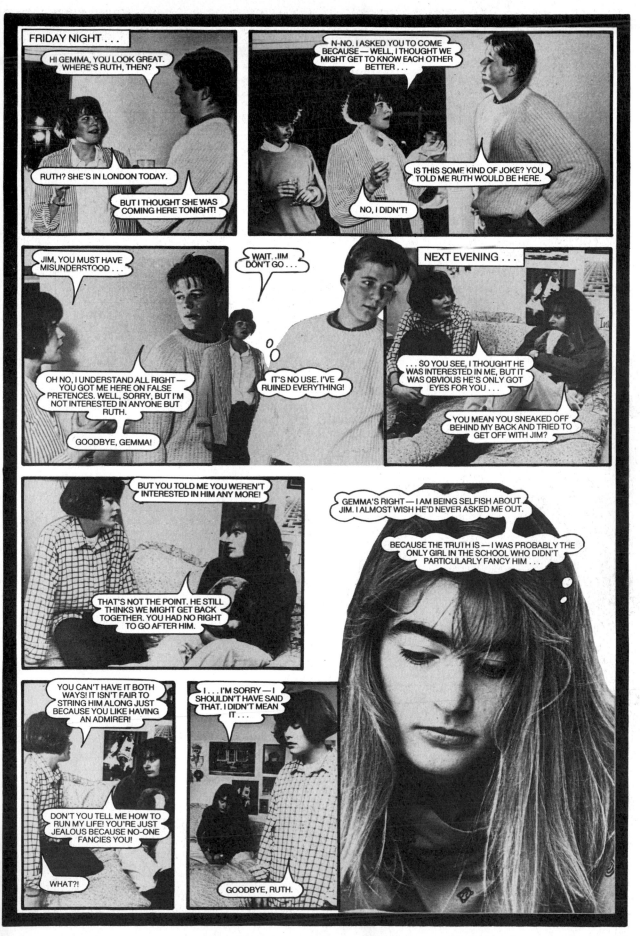

SPECIAL

ALL ABOUT YOU

YOU — AND YOU!

If you don't like yourself, you make it very difficult for others to like you, too. How you cope with any problem often depends on how you feel about yourself to begin with. Once you get in tune with your own personality and capabilities, things can get a lot easier — just read on . . .

As you become more physically and emotionally mature you become more independent and you may find that relationships with people around you begin to alter. These changes can be quite stressful and it helps to remember that others may be experiencing much the same thing and that older people, such as your parents, probably went through similar difficulties growing up.

Thinking about what kind of person you are and about what you'd like to do and be in the future is an important part of learning about your own character and potential. Coming to terms with your developing adult personality can feel lonely and confusing sometimes and you may feel moody and irritable. You'll want to, and be expected to take more responsibility for your own life and actions. This can sometimes cause conflict or self-doubt, after all, you're just starting out and haven't got much experience behind you, but as you adjust you'll find you learn as you go along.

EVERYONE CAN OVERCOME THE MISERY OF SHYNESS

Many young people suffer from shyness or lack of confidence. Remember that others may feel exactly the same, even if they don't always seem to show it. Everyone can overcome the misery of shyness — it's not always easy, but a determined effort should soon bring about an improvement.

For a start, it's no good envying other people or wishing you could be like someone else — you are you and there's nothing wrong with that! Everyone has good qualities and although they may not be patently

obvious at first it's up to you to identify and make the most of them. Maybe you don't feel you're very pretty, have a great figure or are exceedingly clever, but *anybody* can cultivate a nice nature, generosity, good temper, sympathetic manner, etc. These are all much more valuable qualities and will earn you good friends and respect in the long run. Don't underestimate yourself — chances are, if you don't talk about your faults, others won't notice them. They'll probably be too busy thinking about their own! Make the best of yourself and the abilities you do have. Try also, to improve your weaker aspects. If you don't like the way you look, do something about it. Experiment with different clothes, change your hairstyle, or why not write to our Beauty Ed for advice on skin care and make-up? (She's v. good, you know!) If you don't like your figure, work on improving it. Plan a sensible diet or exercise routine and stick to it. With a little determination and effort you should soon see some results.

Capitalise on any talents you have. If you're good at art offer to do portraits or bedroom murals for your mates. If you can cook, help out at local fairs or sales organising the refreshments stall, or offer to help with the food at a friend's party. Those people who're good at sewing would be well appreciated by the local drama group to give a hand ▶

WELL, NO-ONE PROMISED GROWING UP WAS GOING TO BE EASY, BUT SOMETIMES IT CAN BE EVEN WORSE THAN YOU EXPECT! OVER THE NEXT FEW PAGES WE'LL TAKE A LOOK AT SOME OF THE MORE DIFFICULT AREAS OF YOUR TEENAGE YEARS — AND OFFER SOLUTIONS OR ADVICE THAT JUST MIGHT MAKE THINGS A BIT EASIER.

with the costumes. So you see, it doesn't take much to make use of your basic talents and you'll feel a lot better about yourself too.

DON'T FORCE YOURSELF INTO SITUATIONS YOU DON'T FEEL READY FOR

If you're the kind of person who finds it difficult to talk to people or hides away in the corner at parties, then try to take things one step at a time. Start small and gradually build up your confidence until you no longer find it a problem. Don't force yourself into situations you don't feel ready for. It doesn't take much effort to practise saying hello to people, whether it's the paper boy or an old lady in the street. Chat to your neighbours or people you see regularly. Keep an eye on what's going on around you and you shouldn't ever be stuck for casual conversation. Remember too, that you don't have to chatter on ten to the dozen — a few thoughtful comments can be worth a lot more than ten minutes meaningless prattle! People always appreciate a good listener so if you're just not cut out to be the chatter-box type, don't worry about it — you'll be appreciated for your own qualities, in your own right.

It's perfectly natural to feel shy, depressed or doubtful sometimes. It can take a while for your emotions to settle down and for you to come to terms with your changing world. But always remember that you are worth it. Believe in yourself and make the most of all the opportunities open to you. All you need is enough confidence to smile and look friendly — that way you're making it easy for yourself and everyone else!

YOU — AND YOUR FAMILY

When you're young your family can seem like your whole world. But as that world broadens and expands so can the gap between you and your parents . . .

While you're a child you have no option but to live with your parents or as part of a family group, so no matter how difficult things might be sometimes, you've got to learn to get along with them. This isn't just because they're your family: even when you grow up and leave home, at many times in your life you're going to have to be part of a group, whether it's at work, college or sharing a flat with friends. You're going to have to learn how to co-operate, compromise and consider the views of others, so within the family seems as good a place as any to start.

When you're younger, home life can seem like a bed of roses. You're cosseted, looked after and quite happy to muddle along from day to day. It's usually during your teenage years that the problems begin to arise. Suddenly you want to be free, want more independence, want to do as you please without your parents interfering or putting you down all the time. It can be difficult for your mum and dad to accept that their little girl is no longer a child any more and to tell you the truth, a lot of teenagers find it hard to accept themselves. It's all very well demanding to be treated like an adult and thinking that your parents are silly or overly strict but throwing tantrums, having huffs and shouting matches when you don't get your own way isn't going to convince anybody you're mature and responsible.

UNDERSTANDING DOESN'T ALL GO ONE WAY

It's important to keep the lines of communication open. Talk to your parents. If you get into the habit of discussing small problems or upsets it'll be much easier to deal with something bigger if it comes along. Understanding doesn't all go one way though. You've got to be prepared to see things from their point of view as well. It's no good saying 'Oh, but everyone else does' or 'You never let me do anything'. Your parents may have very good reasons for objecting to something. By talking about things calmly you'll begin to understand their worries and perhaps be able to work things out to put their mind at rest.

Your family will accept your need for independence more easily if you show them that you're trustworthy and responsible. If you want to be treated like a young adult you've got to act like one. This means respecting their rules and judgements and not going behind their backs or telling lies. When you are given a little responsibility, use it sensibly. Say you've been disagreeing about staying out late: you want to come in at ten and your parents want you back at nine. If you go out and do as you please, waltzing in at ten anyway, they're not going to trust you again in future, are they? But if you do as they say, act responsibly, they'll see they can trust you and when the subject comes up again they'll be more likely to compromise.

TAKE RESPONSIBILITY FOR YOUR OWN SURROUNDINGS AND BELONGINGS

Growing up isn't just all about freedom and independence. It entails learning to act and think for yourself, as well as others. Once you get a bit older you should be helping more around the house and taking responsibility for your own surroundings and belongings. This means keeping your room and yourself reasonably tidy and not expecting your mum to clean up for you all the time. If you aren't earning money, it's likely that your family will be paying for most of your clothes and stuff and this might also cause a few arguments. It's natural to want to stay fashionable and up to date and you and your mum might not exactly agree on what's suitable and what's not. It's only right though, that whoever's paying should have a say. Anyway, if it was left entirely up to you, chances are you'd end up with a wardrobe stuffed full of snazzy outfits, then moan 'I haven't got a thing to wear', for going to the shops or school! Good quality clothes (the kind your mum likes!), don't have to be unfashionable. A few basic, hardwearing essentials can be dressed up with accessories and combined with other things to make them more adaptable. Remember, it's not what you wear, but how you wear it. Try to come to some arrangement whereby your parents will pay you a small sum each week in exchange for help with the meals, the washing or the housework. Out of this you can save for more extravagant clothes, accessories or make-up. It'll be your money to spend as you like. You might even consider getting a part-time job to boost your funds and it'll show your parents you're prepared for, and can cope with, this kind of responsibility.

COMING TO A COMPROMISE

When it comes to friends and boyfriends your parents might not always agree with your taste, but you've got to remember that you're their

daughter and it's their house and they do have a right to some say over who you go out with or who you invite round. When you make arrangements with friends, check with your mum and dad to make sure they don't clash with other plans they might have. For instance, if your ancient Aunt Edna is visiting for tea, your mum might not be too pleased to have a gang of loud teenagers running up and down stairs!

Inviting a boyfriend round for the first time can be a bit nerve-racking, but there are a few tips to make things a bit easier. It sometimes helps if you can present a guy more as a 'friend' than a 'boyfriend' to begin with, as it'll give your mum and dad time to adjust to the idea of their little girl taking an interest in the opposite sex. Try also, to have something planned, like a visit to the cinema, and leave just enough time for him to pop in for a quick coffee and chat

before you have to go. This should help put your parents' mind at ease over who you're with and how you spend your time, without subjecting the poor boy to a Spanish-style inquisition!

Your home life is a very important aspect of your teenage years and it's worth the effort of making it happy. Your family are the people who love and care about you most, and can provide a comforting refuge when all sorts of other troubles begin to get you down. It's not always easy and there will be times when your views clash or there's rows and arguments. But with a little give and take on both sides, your parents can often turn out to be the best friends you'll ever have!

YOU — AND SCHOOL

You spend an average of seven hours a day at school — it all adds up to quite a large part of your life when you think about it. So isn't it better to keep it as trouble-free a time as possible?

We all have to go to school, at least until we're 16 anyway, so it really is worth making the best of it. Even if you're not very academically-minded, school offers all sorts of opportunities and alternatives. A good education can offer you the kind of freedom later on in life that nothing else can. It can make you strong and independent, not just financially, but emotionally and intellectually. It'll give you the confidence to follow your own preferences and exercise your own opinions.

Most of us run into a few problems at school from time to time: there may be teachers you don't get on with or subjects you don't like. You may feel that certain lessons are beyond you or view some things as being completely irrelevant. Nothing that broadens your horizons or gives you a new insight is irrelevant though. If you feel you can't keep up with a subject or are going to have difficulty with exams, don't be afraid to ask for help. Approach a sympathetic teacher or your guidance tutor and explain your problem. If it's just one specific area, then a few hours extra work, patiently explained to you may be all that's needed to straighten things out. If it's more fundamental than this, they'll be able to work out a sensible plan you can keep up with which should get you back on the right track.

PROBLEMS CAN BE NIPPED IN THE BUD

Even if you do manage to cope with lessons OK, it's still important to stick to a routine of revision and extra study in your own time. Try to spend at least half an hour each evening going over what you've learned that day, making sure you fully understand everything. That way, any problems can be nipped in the bud and you'll have a good grounding for later on. Of course, extra work will be required at exam time, so try to increase your revision appropriately. There's no need to get worked up into a state as exams approach. As long as you have covered all the work and have grasped the essentials you'll do all right. Some people naturally fare better than others, but if you can honestly say you've done your best and tried your hardest, nobody can expect any more of you.

Later on in school you'll have to begin thinking about your options and a future career. Keep an open mind at this stage. It's never too early to start testing the ground, so to speak, so find out all you can about the areas you're interested in. Visit your library or write off to any relevant organisations. You may discover possibilities you hadn't even considered before or see avenues in related fields you didn't know existed. Get all the advice you can. Ask your parents and your teachers, or if you know anyone with a similar job ask them about it.

You may not want to enter straight into a career on leaving school and you may want to continue your education at college or university. It's very important to find out what qualifications you need for entry, if you plan to do this, and make your choices accordingly.

DON'T SUFFER IN SILENCE

Sometimes school life can be made miserable through other things apart from work. Every class will have its

potential bully or trouble-maker and it just takes the right opportunity to bring them out. If you find yourself being picked on then don't just suffer in silence. The quicker you do something about it, the better. The solution depends on what kind of problems you're having. If it's a kind of whispering campaign with unpleasant gossip, scribblings or notes, your best bet is to face up to the people who obviously haven't got the courage to face up to you. Ask them straight why they seem to have it in for you. Don't lose your temper or get tearful — once they see you're not upset, more puzzled, they won't find it such fun any more and will soon move on to something else.

Maybe it's a case of people ganging up on you? Pushing and shoving as you go past? Well don't try to barge your way through, just go a little way off and wait. Gangs seldom have much patience and they'll soon break up and drift off. It's no fun teasing someone who doesn't react. If things are really bad or the physical bullying is getting out of hand, you need more help. Don't be scared to confide in a teacher or your parents — it's not telling tales and a few words in the right direction can make a lot of difference. Don't, whatever you do, try to buy bullies off or give in to their demands. It'll just go on and on and you'll only make things worse in the long run.

SO MUCH CAN DEPEND ON YOUR OWN ATTITUDE

Of course, school life isn't all doom and gloom, it can be a lot of fun as well. You can make new friends, join clubs, go on trips, learn new things, discover new talents and generally take advantage of a lot of opportunities that are open to you. So much can depend on your own attitude at school, so it's important to get it right. School years can be good years, providing a base on which to build the rest of your life. So make the most of school and it'll make the most of you!

YOU — AND YOUR FRIENDS

Sometimes friends can be a pain in the neck, sometimes they can share the happiest times of your life — but where would we be without them? We all need people to share things with, the good times and the bad and sometimes a friend is the only person who can help . . .

Friendships are a very important aspect of your teenage years. Ranging from a casual acquaintance to your closest mate, you'd be pretty lonely without them. At this stage of your life, you'll probably find yourself forming lots of new relationships and growing out of a few old ones. Friends are important for various reasons, you may sometimes feel alienated from your parents, you need someone to share your troubles and secrets, someone who likes the same things as you do and who shares your interests. It's nice to feel that you belong to part of a group and are appreciated for your own identity.

Most of your friends may be made through school but it's a good idea to keep an eye on what's going on elsewhere, too. Youth clubs, leisure centres and hobby groups are all good examples of the type of place you're likely to find others you'd get along with. Ask around or visit your local library or community centre to see what your district has to offer young people. It sometimes helps to have a hobby or interest of your own, that way you can join a club where you're almost sure to meet like-minded people. This is especially helpful if you've just started a new school or moved to a new area. Joining in lunch-time or after-school groups will increase the amount of people you come into contact with and you'll soon find yourself fitting in and settling down.

FRIENDSHIP MEANS GIVING AND TAKING

It's not as difficult as you might think to approach somebody you don't yet know, especially if you have a shared interest. If you're involved in a group or class, comment on how they're doing, ask for a few tips, a bit of advice or generally chat about your chosen activity. Like-minded people are usually drawn to similiar things so the chances are you'll soon find you have a few other things in common as well.

Like most other relationships, friendship means giving and taking. Concentrate on what you put into a friendship, not what you get out of it and the rest should follow naturally. If you give a lot you'll find you get a lot back, and conversely, if you don't, you won't! All friendships go through rough patches, so don't set your expectations too high. Try to deal with problems before they get out of proportion or you can often find yourself trying to remember what the original argument was about in the first place! A lot of friendships get a bit shaky if one of you finds a boyfriend. One of you may be left feeling excluded or neglected. If it's you who gets the guy it's important to encourage your friend to stay involved, confide in her, make time for her when you can give her your whole attention, let her know that she's still very important to you and how much you value her friendship. When you do get together, avoid the temptation to chatter on and on about your boyfriend — she's probably fed up hearing about 'Mr Wonderful'! With a little thought and forward planning you can make time for friends and boyfriends. Just because a friendship slips out of its usual pattern doesn't mean it has to end, it just has to adjust, that's all. When you're younger, friends usually last longer than boyfriends anyway, and they can provide much needed shoulders to cry on from time to time!

DON'T HARBOUR GRUDGES OR RESENTMENT

Sometimes you and your mate can find yourselves after the same guy. Don't let it become a competition. Clear the air and agree to let the best girl win. Harbouring grudges or resentment will only leave you feeling bitter or unhappy. Equally, if it's you he chooses to go out with, don't spend every spare minute talking about him — that's pretty insensitive by anyone's standards.

A friend is someone to lean on, to share jokes with, someone who understands how you're feeling and whose opinion you value. The more friends you have, the busier your social life will be and the more you're likely to meet. So once you establish yourself as a considerate, fun, friendly person you'll find that things just snowball from there. Friendships are important but have to fit into the context of the rest of your life. They shouldn't take priority over your family, school or your own feelings and values. A good friendship will enhance the quality of your life and provide a great refuge from the trials and tribulations of growing up. Many early bonds may last throughout and beyond your teenage years so isn't that something worth working towards? It doesn't take much of an effort to have good friends or to be one. There's an old Irish saying which just about says it all — there are no strangers really — just friends you haven't met yet.

YOU — AND BOYS

With all the problems they cause, it's tempting to think we'd be a lot better off without them! But if you develop the right attitude and keep things in perspective you can save yourself a lot of heartache and get on with the business of having fun!

Love them or loathe them, boys can play an integral part in your teenage years. Suddenly, those annoying little pests who pulled your pig-tails in Primary One can turn into desirable, fanciable beings! When you start to get interested in boys the world can seem like a beautiful place one day and a pain in the neck the next! It helps to remember that boys are human beings too, although you'd hardly think it the way some girls act. What's the right thing to do? What's the right thing to say? What's the right way to act? Well, the truth is there's no 'right' or 'wrong' way to get on with boys. They're people, individuals, just like you and probably suffer all the same feelings and anxieties. Just be yourself.

It's a mistake to pretend to be something you're not. If you force yourself to be the life and soul of the party, you'll probably end up with a really extrovert, loud guy who'll leave you exhausted and disillusioned in a matter of weeks. Same applies if you supress your natural, out-going instincts. You'll probably attract a guy who's pretty quiet and shy himself and who'll bore the pants off you before too long! So be yourself and you'll attract someone who likes *you*.

GET HIM TO NOTICE THAT YOU EXIST

Of course, it's all very well knowing what type of guy is likely to suit you best but how do you get them interested in the first place? There's no guaranteed road to success, but there are a few basic pointers you'd do well to keep in mind. Be friendly. Smile, say hello when you see him. Don't giggle wildly, rush off and hide or stand and stare with your jaw flapping up and down — if he does notice you he'll probably think you're a complete idiot! Try to start up a casual chat: comment on your surroundings, the bus service, the weather — it doesn't really matter, the idea is to get him to notice that you exist. Once you get to know him a bit better it shouldn't be too difficult to drop a few subtle hints about somewhere you'd like to go — the pictures or a club maybe? This way you'll be presenting him with the ideal opportunity to ask you out but you'll have no need to feel embarrassed or rejected if he doesn't.

First dates can be a bit nerve-racking, but remember that the boy is likely to be just as nervous as you. It's quite a good idea to go somewhere, or do something that'll keep you occupied — say ice-skating, a club or a concert. That way you won't be forced into continual conversation and you can avoid any long, awkward silences until you feel a bit more comfortable with each other. Try to keep your sense of humour and just be yourself. After all, he must like you just the way you are to have asked you out in the first place.

NO-ONE CAN SAY WHAT MAKES TWO PEOPLE ATTRACTED TO EACH OTHER

Unfortunately, things don't always work out as we'd like them to. You can't *make* anybody fancy you and you'll have to accept that from the outset. If you don't hit it off or the object of your affections just doesn't seem interested, try not to take it personally. There's nothing wrong with you, it's just the combination that's wrong. No-one can say what makes two people attracted to each other — it's just one of those things. Don't waste time running after someone who obviously doesn't appreciate your attentions — you'll only embarrass them and probably put them off all the more. Know when you're fighting a losing battle, give in gracefully and move on to something else. In a few weeks time you'll probably be wondering what you ever saw in him anyway!

There are occasions where the roles may be reversed and it's you that's not interested. This can be a tricky situation, especially if you still like the boy in question, and don't want to hurt his feelings. The best policy is to be honest and straightforward. The longer you put things off the worse it'll get and both of you could end up feeling bitter or resentful. Just explain how you feel, gently but firmly. Don't write a note or try to tell him over the phone — that's a cowardly way and he'll respect you a lot more if you take the time and trouble to end things gracefully.

THERE ARE LOADS OF NICE GUYS OUT THERE

When you're stuck in a bad relationship it can sometimes take a lot of courage to call it quits. You may feel that you'll never find anyone else or that if you try hard enough, a boy will change his behaviour. That's simply not true. There's loads of nice guys out there but you're never going to find them if you're already attached, are you? If a boy treats you badly, say not turning up for dates, seeing other people behind your back or constantly putting you down it's highly unlikely that he'll change. If you act like a doormat he'll go on treating you like one. If a guy doesn't treat you with the respect and consideration you deserve, then he doesn't deserve you and it's as simple as that.

Teenage romance can provide a lot of good times if you keep things in perspective. It's inevitable that we'll all take a few knocks now and again but the secret is knowing how to pick yourself up, dust yourself down and move on to even better things. You never know just who might be round the next corner! ▶

YOU — AND YOUR BODY

As well as all the emotional changes you go through in your teenage years, your body will be changing too. The complete transition from child to adult takes a few years so use this time to get to know your body, how it works and how to treat it.

From the time you're about 11 until you reach 17 or 18 lots of important things are happening in your life. During this time your body is changing from a young girl's into a young woman's. It's important to have a healthy body which you understand, feel comfortable with and maintain well. The onset of puberty can begin any time from around 10 to 15, so don't worry if you seem to be a little out of sync with your friends or those around you — everyone has their own biological time-clock and things will even themselves out eventually.

Some of the early changes which you may notice are the growth of fine hairs under your arms and between your legs, a sudden spurt in your height, an all-over general rounding of your body and perhaps a milky, white discharge occasionally. These are all just signs that your periods are on their way and it's nothing to be alarmed or embarrassed about. Periods usually occur about once every 28 days although when they first start they may be quite irregular and can take a while

to settle down. Every girl has two ovaries, each one containing thousands of egg cells (ovum). When you reach puberty the egg cells begin to ripen and each month one (or two), the size of a pin head is released and transported though one of the fallopian tubes into your uterus or womb. This journey takes between two and five days and in the meantime the lining of the womb is being prepared for the egg's arrival. It becomes thick and spongey and richly supplied with blood. If the egg cell was fertilised (through sexual intercourse) it would settle there and grow into a baby. If it's not, it disintegrates and is expelled from your body. The unused lining of the womb soon follows and this is what you call your period. Your period may last from two to nine days and some girls lose very little blood while others have a comparatively heavy flow. On average, the blood only amounts to a couple of tablespoons, though it can seem like much more than that.

IT'S REALLY A CASE OF PERSONAL PREFERENCE

These days there's a wide choice of sanitary protection on the market so every girl should be able to find something which suits her. It's really a case of personal preference and each has its own qualities and characteristics. Most girls are given towels by their mums the first few times but it's really up to yourself to decide if you'd feel more comfortable with tampons. Sometimes a girl will have a little difficulty inserting a tampon for the first time and it's not uncommon to find it won't go in or is a bit uncomfortable. Most products usually carry an address where you can write off to for more help or info and it's worth doing this if the trouble continues.

Both towels and tampons should be changed frequently (every four to six hours) even if the flow is light and it's a good idea to carry a couple of spare ones around the time your period's due so you won't be caught out unawares. Many girls find it difficult to approach their mums about this subject but there's really no need to feel embarrassed. It's a natural part of growing up and every woman has periods. Remember, your mum will have gone through much the same things at your age and will be expecting you to ask a few questions sooner or later. It really is a good idea to be able to talk about things openly as many girls get muddled or confused by hearing all sorts of myths or old wives' tales. You *can* have a bath, wash your hair, swim (only if you use tampons), have cold drinks and be as energetic as you like! In fact, having a period shouldn't stop you doing anything you normally do. If your periods are especially painful or causing you problems, don't be afraid to pop along to your doctor. There's no need to feel shy or embarrassed — they deal with things like this every day and can often prescribe something which will help make things easier.

IT'S NATURAL TO FEEL CURIOUS

Of course there's more to growing up than just all this. As you get older you should start to take more responsibility for your own body and well-being. This means eating the right things, taking care of your teeth, skin and hair, getting enough sleep and learning to cope with pressures and demands. It's natural to feel curious about sex and things, but don't fool yourself into thinking that means you're ready to cope with a physical relationship. The legal age of consent is 16 and there are very good reasons for this. When you're younger you're neither physically or emotionally ready for a sexual relationship. Even when you reach 16 it doesn't follow that you have to, just because you can. It's something you should think about very seriously. Taking things further than an affectionate kiss or cuddle should be a shared, loving experience with someone you care about very much, with a mutual trust, understanding and respect. Don't let yourself be pressured into anything you're not entirely sure about. Part of becoming a mature, adult person is learning to set your own standards and values and sticking by them. In the long run, you'll gain a lot more respect from those around you and you'll feel better about yourself too.

There are so many aspects to growing up it's impossible to cover everything at once. But you'll learn as you go along. The main thing is to remember that it's your body and your responsibility. It's got to last you a lifetime so treat it well and it'll treat you well in return.

YOUR BILL OF RIGHTS
I have the right:
To be me
To affection
To love
To support
To ask for help
To be depressed sometimes
To be nervous
To make friends
To be listened to
To say what I feel
To be silly sometimes
To time on my own
To time with my friends
To make my own decisions
To my own values and opinions
To respect
To ask questions
To be angry
To be concerned
To say no

JACKIE
MADONNA

ANNUAL DELIGHTS

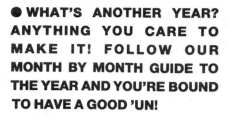

● **WHAT'S ANOTHER YEAR? ANYTHING YOU CARE TO MAKE IT! FOLLOW OUR MONTH BY MONTH GUIDE TO THE YEAR AND YOU'RE BOUND TO HAVE A GOOD 'UN!**

JANUARY

Oh no! It's January, you have no cash left after Crimbo, you've broken all your New Year's Resolutions already, and what's more the Christmas hols are over so it's back to school again. What a start to the New Year!

Cheer up. Here are a few ideas to help you survive until the end of the month . . .

Start a keep fit plan as this is the time to get rid of the flab you've accumulated over the winter.

Hopefully by now, you'll have scoffed the last of your Crimbo sweets so you can give up chocs and sweets, in a bid to clear up your skin and keep the bod in trim.

Treat yourself to a Burns Supper on the 25th. Haggis is sometimes tricky to find in the shops so you may have to make do with the tinned variety, which is much easier to cook anyway. Then all you have to do is peel a mountain of potatoes and turnip and mash them to smithereens.

FEBRUARY

Wow! It's February already. You've actually survived last month's disasters and are ready for all February's festivities. Good! 'Cos here are some of the events you can take part in this month!

The Chinese New Year starts this month. Wey-heh! Why not have a party to celebrate? — To add a bit of extra interest get everyone to dress up as animals from the Chinese Calendar (eg. cats, rats, dragons etc.) and if you can, buy in some Chinese style food — you'll have a rollickin' good time.

Now for Valentine's Day! Start thinking of lots of natty verses to put on your favourite boy's card and, just in case you don't get any, be prepared and send yourself a nice big slushy one. Remember to disguise your writing though — 'cos that way, you'll have everyone fooled!

Oh, mustn't forget Shrove Tuesday on Feb. 16th. Make yourself loads of pancakes complete with maple syrup or lemon juice and scoff them all, while you sit and watch your favourite TV programme. Mind you, don't scoff too many, or you'll have to spend the rest of the month on a diet.

MARCH

Mad March is 'hare'. Woops! I mean 'here'. Ha-Ha! (Groan! Never mind about mad March hares — you're as mad as a hatter! — The Ed.)

Ahem! Talking of Madness, if you happen to be walking along the road on March 17th, and spot a leprechaun creeping past, don't worry, you're not going crazy, (we hope!) — the leprechaun is probably on his way out to celebrate St Patrick's Day, so grab him and take him off to a wild St Patrick's Day party. You've every reason to celebrate you know, as March is the month when we turn the clocks forward and British summertime officially begins. Hooray!

APRIL

Eek! April Fool's Day. Don't let yourself be caught out by little bruv's silly pranks. Instead get smart, plan something naughty yourself and make sure the joke's on him!

April Fool's Day makes quite a good day for organising a sponsored, silly event. Just think, you could have fun doing something crazy and raise money for a needy cause into the bargain.

Don't forget Easter time and all those scrummy Easter eggs you can scoff. Yum. Smartie ones, Mars Bars ones, Milk Tray. Slurp!

Don't eat too many though. You don't want to end up looking like a fat spotty lump for the next few months. Bleee!

MAY

On the first day of May, all girlies are supposed to wash their faces in the morning dew if they want to become beautiful, so why don't you give it a try? Unfortunately, we can't guarantee that this works as ten of us have tried it every year and we still haven't improved! Ha-ha!

Still, you can cheer yourself up by taking part in a May Day parade — you never know you might meet a hunky male under the maypole.

JUNE

Did you know that June 16th 1963 saw the first woman in space? What an achievement eh? Why don't you make June the month to turn over a new leaf?

Decide to get fit. Stodgy, wheezing mass no more! Fitness forever! Yep. Now is the time to take up jogging. Just think of all the lovely males you'll meet as you casually jog through the park during the warm summer nights — sigh!

Another important day in June is Father's Day. You can't forget that, can you? No way. Well, start saving now, or if you're planning to make something — you'd better get a move on. Pamper your dad. (It's not just mums who need looking after you know.) Wash his car or weed the garden for him. Er, it is advisable to find out which plants are weeds and which are flowers before you start though!

JULY

The first week in July sees the last week of Wimbledon. Sob! No more hunky tennis players — oh those tanned, muscley legs. Never mind. Why don't you try taking tennis up yourself? Just grab a friend, two racquets and a ball, and you're all set!

July 4th is Independence Day in America so why don't you have a party to celebrate? Get everyone to dress up as famous American characters and serve everyone popcorn, burgers, candy and Coke. But if you think that involves too much work, just grab a few friends and go down to MacDonalds for a burger 'n' Coke complete with french fries. Yeah man!

Finally, don't forget July's most important event — The Ed's birthday! Yeah! "Cream cakes all round and The Ed's paying!" If you're really bored you can always send her a card, 'cos she doesn't get any from us. Har-Har!

(Thump! — The Mighty Ed.)

AUGUST

Make the most of your summer holiday by getting out and about. If the weather's good, try a spot of camping. Think of the adventures you and your mates could have!

If you feel you'd find going off somewhere a bit too daunting, why not pitch a tent in your garden instead? Then you can invite all your friends round for a sleep-over party. Yo! Zzzzz.

If the weather stays fine, organise a barbecue for all your schoolchums. Though don't forget to send us Jackiettes an invite if you do.

Have a sunbathing party. Ban your brother from the garden and spread out all the chairs, garden loungers and travelling rugs available. Then lay out a stock of sun tan oil, copies of Jackie and lots of cold drinks and ice-cream.

SEPTEMBER

The end of the summer. Back to school. Bah! Gloom! Gloom! Gloom! Well, it doesn't have to be that way. Make the most of the school term. Find out all the various extra-curricular activities school offers. For instance, you might like to join the canoe club, drama group or photography club. You'll make lots of new friends and have quite a bit of fun at the same time.

This is also the month when you should practise bending over backwards to drink your cup of tea, and take your plant pots for walks. OK, people might think you've gone a bit mad but at least you'll brighten up the days!

OCTOBER

The official end of British summertime. Boo! Remember to put your clocks back this month. You don't want to be the only person who turns up at school at quarter-to-eight when everyone else troops in at quarter-to-nine, do you?

Start getting your costume ready for Hallowe'en this month. Make it something really original or really special and you'll be the envy of all your friends.

You could even be making a turnip lantern this year. They're really easy to make. All you need to do is: slice the top off to use as the lid, then hollow out the inside of the remaining turnip. Once you've done that, carve some eyes, a nose and a manic mouth, stick a candle inside and you're all set! Spookity spook!

NOVEMBER

Remember, remember the 5th of November. If you're going to go to an official firework display, put on a pair of of wellies, 'cos these displays are nearly always held in a park or waste ground where the ground is really wet and mucky. Yeuch!

If you, your family or any of your friends are going to be holding a firework display of your own, then please be careful. Make sure you follow the instructions supplied with fireworks carefully and exactly, and stick to the firework code.

Of course Guy Fawkes Night isn't the only occasion you'll have for a get-together this month. The 30th of November is St Andrews day, so why don't you hold a Scottish Day or a Scottish party? You can munch all the lovely Scottish food like tatties 'n' mince, haggis 'n' neeps. Har-har. Bet ye hae a braw time!

DECEMBER

Yipee! 'Tis the season to be jolly. No wonder with all the parties you'll be going to this month — Christmas parties, New Year parties — crisps, mince pies, turkey, chestnuts, Cranberry sauce, sweets, crisps, mince pies, sweets, turkey, mince pies. Burp! Oh the food! The food!

Ah, but don't forget the pressies! Yeah — wait a minute though, we don't just mean the pressies you're going to receive — what about the ones you've got to give out eh? Better write a checklist to make sure you haven't missed anyone out — you don't want anyone to be feeling miffed at you at Crimbo do you? 'Course not!

Talking of forgetting, you won't forget to buy a lickle ol' Advent Calendar will you? Christmas wouldn't be Christmas if you didn't eagerly open the door of an Advent Calendar each day — ooh the nerves! Ooh the excitement! Will it be a picture of a snowman or the stable scene?! Ahh! Sigh . . .

Another thing you might like to know is that the shortest day of the year is around Crimbo time. Wow! Just think — less school!

Well there you are, that's December over! And, hey, guess what? — You've survived the year! Yeah!

I'd Dye

I'M in love with my hairdresser. I mean *really* in love with him. I first spotted him through the salon window, bending to reach the head of a small-insignificant, short-haired girl clad in a red nylon cape. He was razoring the bit at the back, his face set in deep concentration. She stared in the mirror, her face neither happy nor sad, while the razor skimmed her neck. I stood, gawping through the window, when the receptionist caught my eye and gave me a quizzical look. Slightly embarrassed at staring so blatantly, I diverted my gaze and went in.

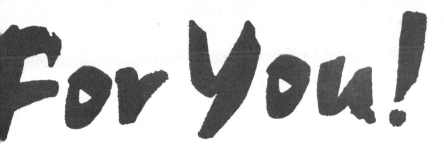
For You!

A hair-raising short story by Fiona Gibson.

"I'd like a haircut, please."

The receptionist eyed my waist-length strands. "You've come to the right place," she murmured through a stifled yawn. She looked at the clock, then met my gaze. "When?"

"Just a trim," I added, "today if it's possible."

She leafed through the appointments book and pencilled my name under the "David" column.

"David?"

"Him," she indicated the tall, dark-skinned, brown-eyed boy dressed in faded jeans and white T-shirt. His hair, short at the back and sides with a long, greased fringe, flopped into his eyes when he bent to trim the insignificant girl's mousey tufts. He stood up straight — six feet of perfect male — and ran gel-covered fingers through the finished result.

"Fine," I said, and homed in on the exit as my temperature rose.

Two hours later, I was installed — afraid to move a muscle — in the very seat of David's last client. Her hair had been swept away and now, my reddish strands were tumbling to the floor. David seemed to prefer silence to smalltalk, and swiftly parted my hair this way and that as he snipped the damp strands. He interrupted the hush only to ask me which bits I'd like to keep and which I'd like to dispose of.

HE WAS SO CLOSE I COULD SMELL HIM.

"Do whatever you like," I croaked, clearing my throat and managing to muster up an encouraging smile.

He was so close I could smell him: a fresh, expensive smell mixed with the gels and sprays of the salon. I reddened, fearful of the vague chance that he might possibly be able to read my mind.

As David's hands stroked the length of my hair, I resisted the temptation to close my eyes. It would have looked silly, after all. But I couldn't help pretending that I wasn't in a salon and David wasn't a hairdresser. I couldn't help imagining that he was running those smooth, brown hands through my hair because he loved me. We were alone, he was caressing my hair (which, in my dreams, was glossy and fair rather

than matted and ginger), and telling me how lovely I looked.

"There," he said. He showed me the back with the aid of a mirror, muttered a curt "OK" as I nodded my approval, and asked for £10.50.

I went back a week later. So far I knew his name, nothing more, so conversation-wise, there was plenty of room for expansion.

"Worked here long?" I asked as he snipped the sides and made squeaky noises with his scissors.

"Weren't you in last week?" he asked, discarding my question like an unwanted lock of hair. "Didn't you like your cut?"

"Oh, no, yes, it was fine. Fine, really. I just fancied going a bit shorter, that's all." So he hacked the back, fiddled with the fringe and gave the whole lot an oily sheen with some funny waxy stuff. I paid my £10.50 and left.

I DIDN'T really want my hair cut any shorter. I'd been growing the stuff ever since my Sindy doll was my favourite possession, and I was quite proud of the fact that my reddish locks acted as a cushion. But, seeing as you can't exactly have your hair cut longer, I decided to go back.

This time I'd talk. I'd ask him about himself. I'd start a conversation, find out what he did after work, and drop hints as subtle as brick walls. After all, hairdressers don't spend their entire existence cooped up in a roomful of driers and basins. No, they go out like everyone else. They have hobbies. They have fun. They have girlfriends.

"You didn't like it," David sighed. I was installed in the seat as he ran his fingers, yes, actually ran his fingers, through the remains of my waist-length hair. Except that now, it barely grazed my shoulders.

"It's still too long," I said, wondering why the salon mirrors made my face look so pink.

"You're crazy," he smiled — yes, *smiled* — as I dug my nails into my palms while hoping he wouldn't chop off the lot.

"Maybe you're right. You'd suit short hair. What's your name, by the way?"

"Julie." I was elated. I knew full well what was coming next. He'd ask me out. Go on, I urged. Ask me. Ask.

"You've got the right shape of face for it," he explained, "so we'll texture the top and feather the sides. Hmm. Strong. Nice."

Whether he meant nice face, nice hair or nice hairstyle, I couldn't work out, but gave him an encouraging smile anyway as he set to work. It was obviously up to me to make the first move. David was shy.

"So what do you do apart from scalp people?" I asked, meaning it as a joke and realising I sounded incredibly pratty.

"Oh, you know — things."

"Me too. I mean . . . uhh. Things. Yes."

MY FRIENDS THOUGHT I WAS MAD.

We fell silent. I paid my £10.50 and left.

My ears were exposed. For the first time since I was wobbling around in Pampers, I could feel fresh air on my neck. My friends thought I was mad. My mum bought me a hat.

OK, so I've gone this far. What's the harm in going shorter? This time I'm going to give it my best shot. Fourth time lucky, that's what I say.

I saunter into the salon with the confidence of a lion. I can't see David, but he's bound to be lurking in the back of the salon.

"You again!" pipes a small, rounded hairdresser with a hairline that's receding faster than my bank balance.

"Been here a lot lately, haven't you? Bit of a regular!"

I nod and scan the salon for David. No sign. "Tell you what," the rounded hairdresser bares his teeth. "I'll save you time. I'll save you time and money, all right?"

"Where's David?" I ask, open mouthed as my head's dipped backwards into the basin.

"Conditioner?"

"Yes, please. Where's David, then?"

"Day off," snaps the rather over-enthusiastic junior.

I'm draped in a red nylon cape, and as the rounded stylist starts to snip, the final remnants of my waist-length hair slip to the floor.

"You want to go shorter?" he asks, his scissors dancing across my hair with all the grace of a combine harvester.

"Yes!" I frown. "No! I just want . . ."

"Lovely," he admires his creation. He strokes the top of my head. It's bristly. I look like a rodent.

"I don't think it's quite . . ." I begin, perspiring profusely beneath the red nylon.

"No, you're right. It needs something else."

A wig, I think to myself. My eyes begin to prick with tears.

"Colour!" he announces. He waves to the over-enthusiastic junior. "Simon, could you get the Bahama Blue out of the cupboard?"

HOLD THE FRONT

... while the Jackie gang get a few exclusive facts on what a day in the life of a journalist is really like. Remember, you read it here first!

"Oh, you're looking for our roving reporter Myrid Ramsay? Mmmm, well I'm afraid she's just rushed off to cover a fire story that came in a few minutes ago. If you're quick you might catch her. Just follow the fire engines and you'll be on the right track!"

Gosh! So *this* is what it's like to be an ace reporter! Oh, well,

Home sweet home — this is where it all happens for Myrid!

best not waste any time ... let's get after the men with the yellow hats and the hose-pipes!

A few minutes later we come across the fire engine and there, sure enough, notebook in hand, is Myrid, getting the low-down on what's been happening in the local pizza house. Luckily it's not a fire after all, just an electrical fault. Phew! You can put the breathing apparatus away now lads!

Myrid's got the story all the same so now it's back to HQ (the Helensburgh Advertiser offices in Scotland to be precise) to find out a little more about what a trainee journalist on the local newspaper actually does every day! ...

"Hmmm, well there's a bit of a problem here 'cos I never really have a typical day! Basically I work from 9-5 p.m. but if something unexpected crops up I could find myself working until quite late at night and in the summer I occasionally have to work over the weekend to cover special events like fêtes and shows that

are of local interest.

"Day to day the work varies all the time according to what's going on in the Helensburgh area. I could end up going to a coffee morning, a fund-raising event or even a burglary ... if one happened at the right time! Usually the way it works is that if you answer the phone, it's up to you to follow up the information that's coming in."

Isn't there a great temptation just to sit back with a cup of coffee and let someone else answer?

"Ha! It never actually works like that in this place. All that would happen is as soon as you went out of the room about a thousand memos would be dumped on your desk and you'd have to get them all sorted out double-quick!

"The start of the week's the worst because we've all got to get the paper to 'bed' — as they say in the trade! — by Wednesday lunchtime. Sometimes it's a real nightmare but Thursdays and Fridays aren't quite so bad — you get a bit more time to get organised."

What happens if you miss a deadline?

"Er, you don't!" ... Myrid giggles nervously as the Helensburgh Advertiser Ed (who doesn't like hammies) appears, as if by magic, in the office.

"No, honestly, we never have too many problems meeting deadlines. As a junior member of staff, if I'm working on a story which I don't think I'll get finished in time I should go to one of the more senior reporters and get them to help me out or at least point me in the right direction. They're OK

about that ... on the whole!

How did you get involved in journalism?

"I'd always wanted to be a journalist when I was at school. I thought it'd be quite glamorous. Ha! Ha! Little did I know I'd spend half my time trudging through muddy fields to get a 'scoop' on some fire that's burned out before I've even arrived!

"I got into journalism in quite a roundabout way. After leaving school I did a two-year course in Communications Studies at Napier College in Edinburgh, then I worked at Channel 5, which is a company that makes promotional videos for advertising companies. I moved on from there, though, mostly because I wasn't getting paid too well (ahem!) then I got into journalism where I get paid even less! Only kidding!

"I actually worked at the Advertiser voluntarily for a few months just to get experience. I wrote in and the Editor got in touch and she told me to come along for an interview. I got on pretty well and liked everybody I worked with, so when I heard that one of the reporters had left to join a radio station I decided to offer my services full time and I was taken on as a proper member of staff."

"Hmm, I wonder if this story will make it to the front page."

Do you think that getting voluntary work experience is a good way to get started in journalism?

"All I can say is that I did and it worked for me. It's good to show that you're keen and if nothing else you get a better idea of what the job actually involves while there's still time to change your mind and think about another career.

"At the moment because I'm still training as a journalist I still go to college to learn all about the legal aspects of journalism and all the other technicalities ... oh, and shorthand. I have to sit a proficiency test after I've completed a set of block release courses at college and by that time I should be up to 100 wpm in shorthand. Er, I'm not very good at the moment, though."

What qualities would you say make a good journalist?

"You have to be willing and able to tackle anything that comes along. There's no point in being snooty about what you want to do, especially if you're just starting out. *Everybody* has to make the coffee!

"Nosiness is also important and being shy is pretty hopeless — there's no such thing as a shy journalist — you have to go into embarrassing situations and learn to cope. I was pretty shy to begin with but I've had to get over that.

"You also have to learn to be smart on the phone because a lot of information comes in that way. I hated speaking to people on the phone when I first started but I'm OK now, in fact I can chat away to people

"OK then lads, where's the fire."

for hours now . . . always about work, of course!

"Being able to talk to and deal with all different types of people is also very important — you have to get people to tell you things or else there'd be no story.

"I've been quite lucky so far because nobody's been really horrible to me when I've gone out to do a story and I think in a lot of situations being female really helps. Oddly enough the most hassle we have is with people coming down to the offices and complaining about their names being spelt wrongly in the paper."

Do you ever run out of questions?

"Yes, it does happen but usually I go out with a photographer and we work as a team, so if I start to dry up a little the photographer usually chips in with something. The photographers here are really nice — apart from Frank, he's OK but he's just got this new jacket that's a little unusual — it's blue and yellow and it makes him look just like one of the corporation buses!" Hmmmm.

What's the most exciting 'mission' you've ever been sent on?

"It was probably over a year or so ago when the Radio 1 team came up to Scotland for a roadshow. They hired a boat and sailed down the Clyde and Wet Wet Wet were the guests. I got to interview them and they all seemed really nice. Mike Read was great too, we had a photographer on board and he was really good about posing for pictures.

"I've been lucky so far 'cos I've never had anything really awful to do. I think the worst thing would be having to 'doorstop' a bereaved family. That happens if we have to do a report on an accident where somebody may have been hurt or even killed. We have to go round to the family's house and speak to them about what happened."

Have you ever had anyone refusing to speak to you?

"It does happen but what we would do in that situation is

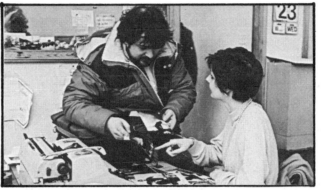
Myrid discusses some shots with one of the Advertiser's photographers.

"What's *this* meant to be!" . . . Myrid's copy gets the once-over from The Ed!

"Oh, no, I've got to phone Buckingham Palace — what if Charles or Di answer!"

run the story and then mention the fact that so-and-so had the opportunity to speak but chose not to comment, which is exactly what happened."

What do you like best about your job?

"Probably the variety, I hate the idea of being stuck in an office all day and it can be quite exciting not knowing what you'll be doing every day. Take today, for instance, there was that fire story to check out and in about half an hour I'll be phoning Buckingham Palace because we've just heard that there's going to be a Royal visit near here soon. This morning I didn't have a clue that any of that was going to happen.

"It's also quite nice to see my name in print. I was really excited the first time I saw my name in the paper under one of my reports — I was buying loads of copies and sending them out to family and friends."

In an ideal world who would you most like to interview?

"Oh, Rutger Hauer . . . he seems really interesting." (Myrid's eyes start to glaze over.)

"I'll tell you what, though, after this I'll be a lot more sympathetic when I interview people . . . All these questions!"

If you're interested in a career in journalism be prepared for a hard slog! Although it's often thought of as an exciting and glamorous job the day to day work of a journalist can be routine and tedious but the competition for jobs on newspapers or magazines is still fierce. You'll have to accept that it'll take a lot of hard work and thorough preparation before you even get an interview!

Check out your local college for Journalism or Communication Courses or try writing to your local newspaper asking if you could see around the offices to find out what goes on. Explain why you think you'd be a good reporter and whether you have a good chance of passing exams. If you're still at school try to do well in English — it's the one subject you must pass to even stand a chance of getting accepted as a journalist.

"Ah, at last, this is what I like best — a quick look at the paper and a nice cuppa."

"Excuse me, sir, if I could just jot down a few particulars . . ."

Myrid sets off on the trail of another 'scoop' in the trusty Helensburgh Advertiser van.

Is She Really Going Out With Him? Wonder where they met? How old is he? How long have they been going out together? . . . These were some of the questions asked when we sent our Jackie reporter out onto the streets to interview innocent young couples about 'going steady' and 'love'.

It must b

Helen 18 and Alex 19

How long have you been going out with each other?
Alex: "Em, nearly eight months."

Where and how, did you meet?
Helen: "We met in John Menzies the stationers — we were both working there part-time. Alex worked in the confectionery dept. and myself in the stationery dept. Both departments were on the ground floor, not much distance apart, so we used to stand at the till points and make faces at each other."

So was it love at first sight?
Helen: "No. For a long time we were just good friends who had a laugh together and shared lunch-hours. It wasn't until I left school and found a permanent job that it all changed. My job was going to be in another town so I had to give up my Menzies job and move away."
Alex: "It was at this point I realised that it was 'now or never'. I found out that Helen was still going to be travelling back at weekends so I finally asked her out — and I've never regretted it yet!"

So is this love then?
Both: "Yes! — definitely."

Do you think it will last?
Alex: "Yeah, I do."
Helen: "I hope so!"

Joyce 17 and Donald 18

How long have you been going out together?
Joyce: "Three months."

Where did you meet?
Donald: "At school. I'm in the year above Joyce but I'd seen her around the school and I'd been to a few parties that she'd gone to, so I knew who she was. Eventually I plucked up the courage to ask her out. I was scared at first in case she said 'No'."
Joyce: "But I didn't!"

Was it love at first sight?
Donald: "Nah! But I did fancy her though. She's got dead nice legs you know."

No need to ask what qualities you find most attractive in your partner then!!
Donald: "Oh, Joyce is good for a laugh too. I like girls with a sense of humour."
Joyce: "Donald's dead nice. He buys me little presents when I'm feeling low and he tells silly jokes to cheer me up as well."

What do you think are each other's bad points?
Joyce: "Football. He goes on and on about football."
Donald: "I do not!"
Joyce: "Yes, you do. You just don't realise it.

Ahem! What about Joyce's bad points, Donald?
Donald: "She's always getting things wrong. But apart from that she's OK."

So do you think you'll stay together then?
Donald: "We'll see."

love!

Beth 17 talking about Darren 17

Beth: "We met on a ferry on the way home from France. We had both been there on holiday — not together I hasten to add!"

Was it instant attraction?

Beth: "Yeah, though all my friends thought he looked like Barry Manilow!"

How long have you been going out together?

Beth: "On and off for 2 years but we only see each other every few weeks as Darren lives a hundred miles away in London. Fortunately he's just passed his driving test so we'll see a bit more of each other when he buys a car."

Is this love?

Beth: "Oh yes! For me anyway. But don't tell Darren I said that."

What do you think Darren's best points are?

Beth: "He's really sensitive. He phones me regularly and he always writes when he says he will."

Does he have any bad points?

Beth: "Weeell, sometimes he can be *too* sensitive. You know, sometimes he's so nice and understanding to me, and I just want an argument. It makes me feel bad afterwards."

Do you think you'll stay together?

Beth: "Who knows? Only time will tell!"

TERENCE LOVES TERENCE

Terence Trent D'Arby and Terence Trent D'Arby (age unknown, because they both keep lying about it!)

Terence has had a long-standing relationship with Terence for as long as they both can remember.

They first set eyes on each other when they both happened to be using the same mirror. It was love at first sight. Neither Terence could resist the other's dashing good looks, charm, wit and fun personality, so they teamed up together and have remained in love ever since. Ahh!

So what qualities do you find most attractive in each other?

"Everything. Terence is just perfect. I love him." Says it all doesn't it?!!

* true love

If you think young love can be strange sometimes, have you ever taken a look at some of the couples you find in the showbiz world? — Well, we've done a bit of research and found some very strange couples indeed!

WHAT A TEAM

Boy George and Mr T (both quite old).

Boy George first met Mr T when George guest-starred in an episode of the A-Team.

Immediately George saw Mr T he was attracted to those big beautiful biceps. (Arm muscles to you non-sporty types.)

Likewise, Mr T couldn't help falling for George when he spotted him wandering around the set wearing one of his natty little frocks. He looked so refined, so delicate. He also admired George's make-up sense too. In his own words, "George is lovely. He's just one big, beautiful bundle of fun."

And what does George think of Mr T? "Worra man!"

CRAZY LOVE

And worra lass our Stacey Smith is. She just can't make up her mind. First of all, she was deeply in love with Paul Young, until Paul decided he was not in love with her, and didn't want her around anymore. (Boo! Hiss!) So, she then flew into the arms of Eddie Kidd. Ahh. Eddie proclaimed his undying love to Stacey and even proposed marriage. But it was not to be. Paul the Pig, decided he wanted Stacey back after all, so Stacey left Eddie in the lurch and hot-footed it back to Mr Bad. Mr Paul 'Bad' Young married Stacey and they had a little sprog. Finally? Well, who knows? — We Jackiettes are so confused with all the to-ing and fro-ing that we're now totally lost. Still that's love, isn't it?

PINKY AND PERKY

Peter Davidson (ageing quite a lot) and Sandra Dickinson (no spring chicken).

Peter met Sandra many moons ago, they fell in love, and married.

True love? Must be. There's no other reason Peter could have stayed with a squeaky dumb blonde and put up with her toy voice for so long.

So what qualities can Ms Dickinson possibly have that keep Peter doting upon her?

Peter: "She's quite a lovable little porker really."

And what about Sandra?

Sandra: "Squeak! I just love it when Peter puts on the little space-age suit he wears when he advertises long-life sauce-pans. It's so dinky. Squeak. Squeak."

*

Well perhaps not *true* love. (Downright lies would be more accurate. Not one single word of this is true! — The Ed.)

Wrong! Boy George did appear in an episode of the A-Team. Har! Har!

THE END 63

THE GREAT
POP & TV & FILM
TRIVIA Quiz!

CONTINUED FROM P12

WHAT'S THE SCORE?

OK, so everybody knows that Sylvester Stallone plays "Rocky", but do you know who provided the ol' bit music for the film itself? Try our little quiz and find out if you're "tuned in" to the movies!

Who performed the title tracks for these here films?!

1. The Living Daylights
2. Rocky (as mentioned above!) III and IV
3. Mannequin
4. Back To The Future
5. Desperately Seeking Susan
6. A View To A Kill
7. Dirty Dancing
8. Flashdance
9. The Snowman
10. Top Gun.

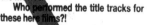

SCREEN TEST

Were you too busy sittin' in the back row, or do you actually remember any of these films which were really popular over the past couple of years?

1. Can you remember the name of the film where Tom Cruise soars through the sky so fast, he takes Kelly McGillis' breath away?
2. An old favourite this one! All about a young lady who ends up somewhere over the rainbow and follows the famous yellow brick road to find her home again.
3. Andrew McCarthy fell in love with a dummy (no, not Samantha Fox!) and lived happily ever after when she came to life!
4. Madonna got an oriental shock when this film flopped!
5. Name the strange laddie who played Michael J. Fox's "pop" in Back To The Future.
6. What's the name of the young, bratette who was "Pretty In Pink"?
7. Name three members of the Brat Pack who were in the movie St Elmo's Fire.
8. How many dwarfs were there in Snow White And The Seven Dwarfs?

CONTINUED OVERLEAF

THE GREAT POP & TV & FILM TRIVIA Quiz!

"WHAT'S IN A NAME?"

Ever wondered where bands get their sometimes incredibly odd names from? You do? Good! Try your luck with the next little teaser then. Where do they get those names?

1. Wet Wet Wet
2. Bros
3. Dire Straits
4. Five Star
5. Johnny Hates Jazz
6. Depeche Mode
7. Duran Duran
8. Pepsi and Shirlie
9. Marillion
10. The Pogues
11. The Two Ronnies
12. Simple Minds.

ON THE BOX

1. What did Gareth Hunt do before he made the acclaimed Nescafé ads? He appeared in TV crime-busting progs. — but do you remember his most famous?
   a) The Proclaimers
   b) The New Avengers
   c) Queen's Park Rangers!
2. Who is the guy who wears the sharp suits and has a lovable lisp, you know: "Hewo, Good Evening and Wewcome to The Wast Wesort!"?
3. Smarties are kept in this, it was also a v. popular Channel 4 pop programme.
4. Bruce Willis is a singer sometimes, but do you know the name of his fast talking character who does a bit of Moonlighting?
5. Which "soap" features the characters Amos, Mr Wilkes and a few hundred sheep?
6. On what show can contestants have a "P", as long as they ask Bob?
7. Which show was the character Damon Grant featured in?
8. Zippy, George and what's the other bloke in Rainbow called? (No, not Jeffrey!)
9. Who is Nerys Hughes?
   a) The Bionic Woman?
   b) The District Nurse?
   c) A Radio 1 DJ?
10. Can you remember the first Saturday morning programme, long before Saturday Superstore or Going Live were but a twinkle in the BBC's eye?

"PLAY IT AGAIN, SAM."

You've heard the tune, but do you know the songs these following lyrics come from?

1. "De Do Do Do De Da Da Da"
   Clue: Also known as the "Old Bill".

2. "She used to be a Diplomat, but now she's down in the laundromat.
   (Brilliant rhyme this!)

3. "Sometimes you're better off dead, there's a gun in your hand it's pointing at your head, you think you're mad, too unstable, kicking in chairs and knocking down tables..."
   (zzzzz — hurry up!)

4. "Bathgate no more,
   Linwood no more,
   Methil no more,
   Irvine no more!"

5. "When I give my heart, it will be completely,
   Or I'll never give my heart,
   And the moment I feel that you feel that way too,
   Is when I fall in love with you.
   (awww!)

✳ ✳ ✳

C O N C L U S I O N S

Give yourself 1 point for each correct answer, and 12 points for correctly completing the wordsearch.

90-120
Well, well, well! We ARE a clever trousers, aren't we?

Are you sure you didn't cheat? You didn't! Congratulations are in order then — you are truly a trove of trivia treasure. Perhaps even more intelligent than the Jackie staff. (Wouldn't be difficult! — The Ed.) I'll bet you even know whose idea it was to put the tiny holes in the sides of biros! Advance to Mayfair and collect £200!

60-90
Well done! You waded your way through the trivia and managed to come out with a very respectable score. You obviously know your Tom Cruises from your Gareth Hunts. Why, you'll be the envy of all your friends when you tell them your score. Ahem! Don't worry if you don't have a clue about holes in biros, you're still a whizz at the trivia that REALLY counts!

30-60
Erm... not very "tuned-in" to the trivia wavelength, are you? Never fear! There's more to life than scoring highly in a truly wonderful Jackie quiz, but not much (har! har!). Get yourself down to your nearest friendly bookstore, (see Yellow Pages!) and discover some "interesting" books like — "Gareth Hunt — Everything You Ever Wanted To Know, But Couldn't Be Bothered Asking". Joking aside, you made a fair attempt, but you must try harder!

Under 30(!)
Hmm... Where HAVE you been for the past squillion years — Darkest Peru? Even if you guessed the answers how could you possibly get such a low score? You should be ashamed! Never darken the pages of this quiz again — at least until you've learned all the answers "off by heart" and can recite them backwards standing on your head!

LET'S MAKE-UP!

After going bare-faced throughout the summer it's time to reach for your make-up bag again. Don't plaster it on any old way, though — stick to a simple routine for a flawless finish . . .

1. Cleanse, tone and moisturise your skin.
2. Cover up any dark circles, spots or blemishes by dabbing on a little cover stick.
3. Carefully blend foundation over your face and throat making sure you don't leave any harsh lines.
4. Finish off your base with a light dusting of a loose translucent face powder.
5. Now give your face some shape by applying a little blusher. Don't go overboard — start by applying just a little and building up to the depth of colour you require.
6. For eyes stick to just a few of your favourite shades and blend together carefully with a fine make-up brush. To give added definition outline the lower rim with eyeliner and apply a couple of coats of mascara.
7. Emphasise your lips with a slick of lip gloss or lipstick. When applying lip colour outline your lips first with a lip pencil then fill in with colour. Blot your lips on a clean tissue, re-apply, then blot again for extra staying power.

HALLOWE'EN TOP TEN

1. Bat Out Of Hell — Meatloaf
2. Devil Woman — Cliff Richard
3. Ghost Train — Madness
4. Every 'Witch' Way But Loose — Eddie Rabbit
5. Who's That Ghoul? — Madonna
6. Scarey Monsters — David Bowie
7. Ghosts — Japan
8. The Devil Went Down To Georgia — The Charlie Daniels Band
9. Spirits In The Material World — The Police
10. Ghost Town — The Specials.

WHAT THIS SEASON HAS IN STORE
AUTUMN GO

HEALTHY HAIR

If the summer sun has caused havoc with your hair then now's the time to do something about it and get it in top condition again . . .

● When washing your hair choose a shampoo for your particular hair type and always rinse off thoroughly.

● Get your hair trimmed regularly to ward off split ends.

● Try a deep conditioning treatment and wrap your hair in warm towels while you're waiting for it to work.

● If you use a hairdryer to dry your hair then keep it moving at least six inches away from your hair and at a low heat setting.

GLOWING PLACES

If you've worked hard all summer to get a glowing tan then you won't want it to fade as soon as the sun disappears!

Make it last as long as possible by having showers instead of baths and moisturising your skin with a good body lotion after every one.

Treat yourself to a few sunbed sessions or invest in some fake tan. As long as you apply it properly no-one should be any the wiser!

You can keep that bronzed look for your face too by using a tinted moisturiser or by subtly blending in a little cream blusher in a tawny or golden shade.

SHADES OF AUTUMN

Changing your hair colour needn't be a hair-raising experience as long as you follow all the instructions very carefully.

Wash-in wash-out hair colours are the simplest to use — just shampoo in, leave for the required length of time, then wash out. If you don't like the new shade, don't panic — you can wash it out again.

For a longer-lasting effect there are several semi-permanent colourants available. Read the instructions on the pack very carefully and, if required, do a skin test. Never colour your hair if you've just had a perm — that's just asking for trouble!

Permanent colourants are just what they say — permanent, so don't be tempted to experiment — leave that to the hairdresser.

D!

PET SHOP BOYS

summer loving

PICS BY RICARDO GUIRALDES

71

74

CONTINUED ON PAGE 92

A NIGHT ON THE TOWN

Big date? Tune into our step-by-step beauty routine and knock 'em dead!

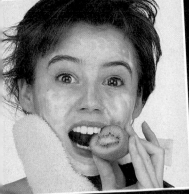

The big night's finally arrived. The bedroom's heaped up with discarded outfits and right this minute good ol' Mum's frantically mending the zip on that vampish red dress you'd forgotten you had.

You've got exactly an hour or so to create Vampy Veronica from Schoolgirl Susie so you'd better get cracking!

Make a start by removing all traces of make-up then relax for ten minutes in a scented bath. It'll leave you feeling like a million dollars.

Next you'll have to make sure he can run his fingers through your clean, fresh-smelling hair, so get washing. Once it's squeaky clean, brush your hair until it's tangle free then pull it back from your face until you've finished your make-up.

Not only will that bath have made you smell sweet, it's also prepared your skin for a thorough cleansing.

Cleanse and tone using upward strokes so's you don't get wrinkles, making sure you leave no trace of lotion. Complete your routine by moisturising your skin. You'll find your foundation will smooth on much more easily.

If you have any spots, now's the time to hide them with a medicated coverstick, remembering to blend it in well.

Your foundation should be as close to your natural skin colour as poss. Use it sparingly and blend it in too. There's nothing worse than an orange line around the chin! If your skin's clear you might not even need to cover your whole face. Just touch up your nose, chin and forehead. But make sure you're working in a good light or else you'll end up with two-tone make-up.

Be as adventurous as you like with eye make-up, especially if he's taking you somewhere glam. But make sure you've experimented before the big night — tribal warpaint won't get you another date, that's for sure. If you're in doubt, choose an eyeshadow to match your outfit and apply it over the whole lid. Apply a slightly darker colour to the outside corner and add a little highlighter just below your brow bone. It's as simple as that.

A kohl pencil will look great smudged around the outside corners of your eyes, and a little mascara on the lashes will add that final touch. Go for a bright shade if you dare. Remember, your eyes convey your feelings.

The next step to looking thoroughly delectable is applying your blusher. It's not as difficult as it sounds.

Just suck in your cheeks and apply the blusher to the bit which you can still see — i.e. your cheekbones. Don't make the lines too harsh though. Taking a large brush, blend the edges into your foundation. You might like to use a pearlised highlighter just above the cheekbone for a really special occasion.

A slick of lipstick, co-ordinating with your eyeshadow of course, puts the finishing touches to your magic make-over. Line your lips with a lip pencil if you're worried about 'bleeding', then, using a special lip brush to give you an even coverage, smooth on some colour, blotting the excess on a tissue then apply a little more. A tasty lip gloss will give you those film star looks. Aah, the perfect pout! If he doesn't fall at your feet now, he never will.

All that's left is to dry off your hair, maybe jazzing it up with a few bright accessories — bows, headbands or even flowers. Maybe a friend would help you blow dry your hair into a really sleek evening style or if you have curly hair scrunch dry it for a wildcat look. Take a handful of hair, scrunch it into your hand then blow dry that small section. A quick scoosh of hairspray will hold it in place but slip a handbag-sized spray in your bag just in case of a hurricane.

All that's left is to squeeze into your slinky number and sneak out before your mum catches you. Have an ace night!

SNOOPY VERSUS THE BISTRO KIDS

specially written for Jackie by **Cathy Young**

BEING called Charlotte was bad enough, but Charlotte Brown . . . I don't know what my parents were thinking about when they christened me. Charlotte had been shortened to Charlie, and then to —yes,you've guessed it — Snoopy. I'd just got myself a part-time job at The Bistro, this dead trendy restaurant in town, and the last thing I wanted was for everyone to call me Snoopy. It was such a stupid nickname.

One of my mates' big sisters had worked in The Bistro before she left to get a job in London somewhere. As soon as Sarah said that her sister, Kay, was leaving I decided I'd ask her to put in a word for me.

I WAS ALREADY PICKING HOLIDAY ITEMS.

I wanted the job pretty badly, because I'd decided I wanted to go to Corfu in the summer. I was already picking holiday items from Mum's catalogue. There was a fabulous black swimsuit with really high-cut legs and an equally low-cut top that I knew I had to have. Little Snoopy would make the locals sit up and take notice in that. It was dead expensive but I reckoned I'd soon manage to save that up when — or if — I got Kay's old job.

I pestered her for a whole week before she finally agreed just to even mention that she knew someone who was looking for a job. And after all those times I never let on she had boyfriends round when she was supposed to be babysitting for me when I was a kid. (Well, two years ago actually. My mother always thinks mad axemen are going to break in, or the house is going to catch fire whenever she and dad have left the place for five minutes.) I had to threaten to explain to my mum exactly how the glass-topped coffee table got cracked or how the cigarette burn on the carpet had really got there before she agreed.

The next Wednesday, Kay came round to tell me I was to start that Friday. "The only reason you're getting this job is as a favour to me, because you're my sister's mate, so don't do anything stupid," she said glaring at me. "And don't mention you're still at school either. I had to lie and say you were 18 and at college. You'd never have got it if they knew you were only 15."

"16," I corrected.

"Well, whatever. Just don't show me up."

THE BISTRO was a big disappointment. It was a lot tackier than I thought, for a start, and the owner didn't look anything like I'd imagined.

"When Kay first came she started serving straight away," she told me, "but I think we'd better give you a trial first, helping behind the counter. OK?"

When I got fixed up with a uniform — a very short bleached denim skirt and a big baggy T-shirt — I wished I'd been to Corfu already so my pasty-white legs looked a bit better.

Several hours later I'd mopped floors, washed dishes, cleaned ash-trays, emptied rubbish bins, swept up two broken glasses and — the highlight of the evening — folded a bundle of tacky green napkins — the only job that didn't involve me getting filthy or up to my elbows in detergent.

THE TIPS CAME TO A GRAND TOTAL OF ZILCH.

While I'd been busy slaving away, Teri and the rest of the staff — Roz, Shirley, Jenny and a rather gorgeous bloke called Sebastian — had all been swanning about chatting to customers and replacing the occasional cappuccino (they didn't serve ordinary coffee at The Bistro), straightening chairs and generally posing about. They were all dead keen to serve customers and give them a bit of chat, because you kept all your own tips and if you hadn't served anyone — like me — all the huge tips that Kay used to go on about came to a grand total of zilch.

Three weeks later, nothing had changed. I was still getting all the grotty jobs.

The other girls hardly talked to me, and when they did it was to slag me about my hair, make-up and everything else and just generally make my life miserable. If it hadn't been for the fact that I knew Sebastian would be there, I would have dreaded going in every Friday and Saturday night.

Sebastian was brilliant. He was the only one who spoke to me, and he was really good-looking. He was quite a bit older than me, but I thought he quite liked me. He wouldn't have spoken to me otherwise, would he?

Of course Sarah and everyone from school thought I was having a brilliant time. People kept coming up and asking me what it was like

to work in The Bistro. I didn't really mean to lie but one thing sort of led to another until it was all around the fourth year that I was earning loads of money and was practically going out with Sebastian.

A COUPLE of weeks later I heard Teri tell Shirley that Kay was back for the weekend and that everyone from The Bistro was going out after work the next day. Now was my chance to impress Sebastian and to show Teri and the rest of them that I could be just as glamorous and sophisticated as they all thought they were.

Sarah and I had already arranged to go shopping that Saturday morning. Sarah wanted a new pair of jeans for Tracey Smith's birthday party. It was going to be the first party I'd not been to with Sarah and everybody from school, but I was working. I think Sarah was a bit miffed when she knew I was going out after

"What's more," Roz giggled, "she's forgotten about the price-tag and Sebastian's hidden the scissors so she can't cut it off!"

"It's going to be hilarious seeing her face when she gets all dolled up only to get knocked back at the club," Sebastian butted in. "They're never going to let her in dressed like that. What an embarrassment!"

MY face was still burning, but not with embarrassment — with anger. They'd been so intent on slagging me off that none of them had seen me at the door so I went back to the toilets, bundled all my stuff back into my bag, took a deep breath and walked back into the restaurant.

They were totally knocked back when they turned round expecting me to make a complete twit of myself, only to see me standing in the doorway wearing a jumper and my uniform denim skirt.

"Right," I said sounding far more confident than I felt. "I'll just get my handbag and I'll be off. 'Bye."

"Where are you going?" asked Roz, sounding surprised.

"My friend's having a party," I said. "See you next Friday."

The party was still going strong when I reached Tracey's house. I suddenly remembered I didn't have a birthday present for her so I dived into my bag for the new make-up that I'd bought.

Sarah was really surprised to see me — and to see I wasn't wearing the new dress. She could see I was upset about something and soon got the truth out of me. I tried to tone down the bit about Kay being such a bitch but they were sisters so I suppose she had a fair idea anyway.

"I thought it was all too good to be true. Anyway, it's nice to get the old Snoopy back. You've been a real pain this last couple of weeks."

"I've had a miserable time. I've made a complete idiot of myself — and you know what makes it worse? I haven't even made any money out of it," I moaned. "I spent all my wages on that stupid dress which I hate and I'll probably never wear."

"But if you've not cut off the price tag, you can return it and get a refund. That shop takes things back no hassle. See, things aren't that bad," Sarah smiled. "And when we're returning the dress, why don't we both go into that burger place next door that Craig works in and see if we can get a job? Can you imagine you and me in those stupid little caps squirting tomato ketchup at each other? It'd be a laugh."

"Yeah, but Craig only gets £1.50 an hour. I'm never going to get to Corfu on wages like that, or get that swimming cossie or any decent clothes . . . still, it would be a laugh, wouldn't it? Fancy Blackpool instead of Corfu . . . ?

THE END

---

work but I couldn't manage the party, but when she saw how determined I was (the fact that I blew all of the last three weeks' wages on a clingy black dress and some new make-up went some way to persuading her I was serious) she started to get a bit excited too, although she didn't really like the dress.

They all seemed to be pretty amazed when I appeared that Saturday night with my bag packed with my new dress. They'd probably thought I wouldn't be allowed out so late. I wasn't, actually, but I thought the row would be worth it.

Kay arrived at eleven o'clock just as the last customers were leaving. I left Kay telling everyone about how wonderful the big city was and went into the toilets to get ready. I'd had a quick wash and had taken my T-shirt off when I realised I'd left my handbag with all my make-up in the restaurant, so I pulled my jumper back on and went to pick it up. As I

opened the restaurant door I could hear them all laughing.

"When she appeared with that big bag tonight I could have died," Teri was saying. "I knew she was listening to us when I was telling Shirley about the club the other day."

"That's all we need," laughed Sebastian. "Charlotte tagging along!"

More laughter. I could feel my face burning.

"THEY'RE NEVER GOING TO LET HER IN DRESSED LIKE THAT."

"What a way to talk about your girlfriend! She fancies you rotten, Seb. It's so obvious! And that bag!" Teri said. "Have you seen what's in it? It just *happened* to come unzipped when Roz and I were on our break in the staff room. She's got this hideous black thing straight out of Joan Collins' wardrobe!"

Testing, Testing,

Frankie: Frankie has quite rosy cheeks and found that her make-up started to slide off during the disco, no matter how carefully it was applied.

Overcoming the problem of rosy cheeks is made simple by using

colour corrective foundation, which costs the same as a normal foundation — the main difference being that it's green in colour! Don't let that put you off, though. It's used under your normal make-up and you WON'T end up looking like an extra from a horror movie! Simply apply after cleansing and moisturising and leave to dry for a few minutes before making up as normal. As you can see, the results were simply stunning and Frankie's opinion — "It's really brill. The difference is unbelievable — definitely something I'll buy in future."

Most girls buy make-up, moisturiser or mascara at some time or another. You know the routine — into Boots, up to the cosmetics counter, pick out your usual "shade", pay for it and walk out happily. There are, however, a few things which you might not normally buy on your soujourn to Boots. We grabbed five "volunteers" to act as our guinea pigs (hamsters if you prefer) — and here's what happened.

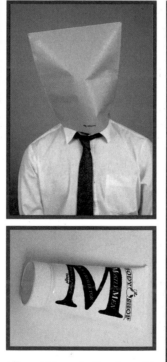

The Steve!: You could do your boyfriend a BIG favour if you buy him some of the men's beauty products available in the shops just now. Although they may think things like moisturiser are "girly", they'll soon notice the difference when they start using them! We talked Steve into trying out a men's moisturiser from The Body Shop. He wasn't too keen at first — but, as you can see, it softened his paper bag enough to make him crack a smile! He recommends that all boys use moisturiser, as it improves their appearance. It really has done a lot for Steve — snigger!

1, 2, 3... er 4, 5!

Pauline: Pauline was asked to test a "cheap" foundation and an expensive one to see if the extra pennies were really worth it. The expensive foundation was hypo-allergenic, which means it's very good for girls who can't wear certain kinds of make-up because of the perfume in them or other ingredients. Our cheaper foundation did have a slight perfume to it. Pauline tried both, and liked them both — however, she couldn't really feel much difference in them. They were both easy to apply and felt nice on, although the expensive brand did tend to feel a bit heavy. Did she think it would be worth splashing out on a more costly foundation? — "It would be fine for people with allergies to make-up, but I didn't really notice a big difference, actually! I think I'd stick with the cheaper one."

Shirlie: Shirlie was persuaded to try out what looked like instruments of torture. They are, of course, eyelash curlers and don't let their appearance put you off. Eyelash curlers are for people who don't like messing about applying three coats of mascara first thing in the morning. To use them, simply press them open and hold them near your eyelid until they are covering your eyelashes, then slowly close the eyelash curlers together. Hold them like this for a count of 30 — release — and voilà, curly eyelashes will be yours!

Of course, you could apply a light coating of mascara after using them to ensure maximum effect, but they are good for girls who don't like using mascara. Also, if you carry them when you go out, your eyelashes can quickly be re-curled when needed! What did Shirlie think? "I was a bit put off at first by the way they looked, but when I tried them, they curled really well. I would still put a light coating of mascara on top to colour my lashes."

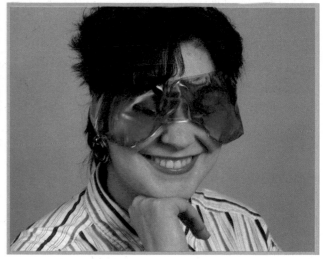

Tracey: Like most girls, Tracey loves a night on the town. She doesn't love the way she looks in the morning, though! Let's face it, having saggy eyes which resemble pillows isn't very attractive at all. Cool pacs for the eyes are an excellent invention for the "Just got out of bed and can't wait to get back" look. You can keep your cool pac in the fridge and it can be used again and again. It only takes around 15 minutes to revive your eyes and doesn't have to be used in the morning. You can have a relaxing lie down before you get ready to go out and ensure you look as "fresh as a daisy"! So, did it manage to wake Tracey up? "I felt really relaxed after I used it and it made a real difference to my eyes. Not something I would have thought about buying before, but I wouldn't be without it, now."

Well, girls, now you know — there are a lot of beauty products you may not have thought about before. This feature has shown you a few, but remember to keep your eyes open for any new products which appear on the market. You never know — they could make all the difference!

FIRST AID

A "Useful" Guide To First Dates!

Yippee! You've made a date with HIM to go to the pictures. It's your first date with him, he's really nice, oooh . . . But, wait! There are at least three hundred things you can think of that could go wrong — ooer, read on, all will be revealed in this fun feature about first dates!

"Erm . . . I was wondering if maybe you'd like to, er . . . go to the pictures on Saturday night, Trace?"

"Er . . . OK Trev, sounds brill!"

So, maybe you're not called Tracey or Trevor but how many times have you been asked out on a "date"? You're pleased that the guy you've fancied for ages has finally asked you out, but then the problems start! What will I wear? Where will we go? What can we talk about? What if we don't like each other? Will we kiss each other? Then the real worry — what if he doesn't turn up?!!! Don't worry — read on and discover that a first date doesn't necessarily mean your first nervous breakdown!

What To Wear

The first thing to do is decide what you're going to wear. After all, there is no

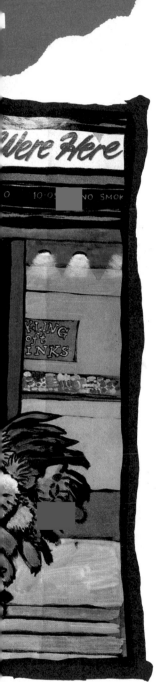

take time to apply your make-up. Take a look in a full length mirror and check the way you look before you leave home — make sure you feel comfortable when you leave the house, as this is the first step to enjoying yourself.

Where To Go

When you reach the place you arranged to meet, don't be alarmed if the wonder boy isn't there — he will be ! (Well, normally boys do turn up!) If you haven't decided where to go and he asks you, don't stand there saying "I dunno, it's up to you" . . . this is pointless and will only make him think you are an idiot. Instead, keep a few suggestions in mind, the obvious ones are the cinema or the café in the local sports centre! You should be able to come up with somewhere between the two of you. If, on the other hand, he gives you a choice between watching him and his mates play snooker or watching him and his mates play five-a-side, then, well, he's probably not the boy for you, unless that kind of thing appeals to you. If you decide to go somewhere that requires money to get in, the best thing to do is offer to pay half, even if he doesn't take the money! This could also be awkward, because he may be offended at you offering to pay, then again, if he doesn't have a lot of money, he may be glad of it! So, at least offer the money, he'll decide what to do about that.

What To Say

Assuming that you've found somewhere to go and you've managed to sort out who's paying (it's not as complicated as it sounds!) you do have to talk to each other. What do you talk about? Occasionally, you go out with someone you hit it off with right away and the conversation just flows. However, most times you do have to think before you speak! The first thing to do is avoid pressing your views on him, don't act as though you're on a crusade when you are having a discussion! Another thing to do, is avoid discussing ex-boyfriends, this IS a mistake. Resist the temptation to make an amusing comment about a rather large girl's taste in clothes as she walks past — you don't want him to think you're bitchy! Stick to "safe" subjects like school/college, music, TV, films and mutual friends.

The Kiss!

If all of this goes to plan and the date is nearly over, the next thing on your mind is whether or not he will want to kiss you! Don't worry about this, let things take their course — and don't be expecting the kiss to sweep you off your feet when it does happen! You do have to practise things to get them right!

You're at your door and he's said goodnight, you're about to go in when — "Erm . . . what about coming out on Tuesday, Trace?"

If this doesn't happen, don't panic!

Will He Ask Again?

So, you enjoyed yourself, he was good company, you seemed to like each other . . . What has gone wrong? Well, there could be a number of things! He may not want to seem too keen, he may only like taking girls out for one night. There is always the possibility that he is shy, even though you've been out together already! Maybe he's unsure of the way you feel. Whatever the reason, you're now standing guard over the phone and anyone who mentions his name is interrogated for info. If you know that there is a possibility that you will see him during the day, it is advisable to take such an opportunity. If you bump into him, smile, and start a friendly conversation — if he doesn't respond then that's it — forget it! He is obviously not worth bothering about.

If, on the other hand, you don't want to talk to him yourself, grab a friend, who you know well and who knows the boy himself! Bribe her with sweets, tears or a promise to babysit her horrible brother for the next six months! She could just ask him how things went, and if he wants to see you again.

He may be worried that you'll say no or, indeed, he may not want to appear too keen (boys are real creeps, eh readers!). Don't ask him out, just say "Well, I suppose I'll see you soon," or something like that!

But even best friends aren't always to be trusted, so be careful who you choose to act as a go-between.

If all this fails (it better not! — The Jackie office) then there are three things you can do to cheer yourself up. First of all, visit your friendly sweet shop and stock up on an enormous supply of sweeties. Secondly, slump in front of the TV munching merrily and moaning at EastEnders. And last, but not least, march off down to the youth club/sports centre/ice rink and find yourself a new boy!

point in getting glammed up in six inch heels and a little black number for a walk in the park! If you don't know where you're going on your date, then stick to something plain and practical — like a shirt and a pair of trousers or jeans. Keep make-up subtle too, you don't want to look as though you work behind the cosmetics counter at Boots! Leave yourself plenty of time to get dressed, lay your clothes out washed and ironed, ready to put on — then

CHINESE-SCOPE
— we take a Pe-king to your future!

If you're a bit of a Snake, 1989 is your year but all you Rats, Tigers, Dragons . . . don't despair, our resident Chinese astrologer, the famous and incredibly talented Steve Le Chow Mein has got you well-sussed!

If you check out Teenscope in Jackie every week you'll be well familiar with our Western horoscopes, but did you know there was a whole other set of horoscopes? It's based on the Chinese horoscope system which is thousands of years old. This system is pretty straightforward — years are divided into groups of twelve and each of these years is assigned the name of an animal. The ancient Chinese reckoned they could tell a lot about the kind of character a person would have according to which animal sign they were born under.

This all started when, according to legend, many, many years ago, Buddha summoned all the animals in his kingdom to his side but only twelve turned up. Buddha was understandably a bit miffed by this, so to reward the faithful twelve he awarded each one of them a year of the Chinese calendar. The rat was the first animal to arrive at Buddha's side so he was given the first year. The sequence is always the same and runs as follows: Rat, Ox, Tiger, Cat, Dragon, Snake, Horse, Goat, Monkey, Rooster, Dog, Pig.

To find out your Chinese horoscope sign, simply look up the year of your birth in the list and remember that the animal characteristics are v. strong in people born at the beginning of the year but get weaker as the year progresses. (If you want to work out which animal sign older members of your family are, all

you have to do is work back through the animal sequence to the year of their birth eg., if you have a 20-year-old brother he must have been born in '69, we know from the list below that 1971 was the year of the Pig, two signs back in the animal sequence tells us that your brother would have been born under the sign of the Rooster! Note: you have to be careful with people born in January or February because the Chinese year differs in length and the first day of the New Year could occur anytime between mid-January and mid-February.)

THE CHINESE YEARS

February 6, 1970	—	January 26, 1971	...... Dog
January 27, 1971	—	January 14, 1972	.... Pig
January 15, 1972	—	February 2, 1973	.... Rat
February 3, 1973	—	January 22, 1974	.... Ox
January 23, 1974	—	February 10, 1975	.... Tiger
February 11, 1975	—	January 30, 1976	.... Cat
January 31, 1976	—	February 17, 1977	Dragon
February 18, 1977	—	February 6, 1978	... Snake
February 7, 1978	—	January 27, 1979	... Horse
January 28, 1979	—	February 15, 1980	..... Goat
February 16, 1980	—	February 4, 1981	Monkey
February 5, 1981	—	January 24, 1982	Rooster

THE RAT

If you were born under the Year of the Rat you'll be a real charmer! Intelligent, popular and sociable, you'll love attending parties just so you get a chance to sparkle in front of a big bunch of people. You make friends really easily but although you like people, you don't really trust them and you keep a lot of your deeper feelings to yourself.

You are hard-working and ambitious and you'd think nothing of using the famous Rat charm to use people to get what you want. Nasty, nasty! Rats are usually very observant and make good writers or journalists. They also do well in public relations and personnel because they're good at dealing with people.

Rats are very family orientated and will do whatever they can to help out their loved ones. Although they can sometimes seem a little mean with money they are always v. generous with their family and close friends. They can also be pretty extravagant with themselves. If you're a Rat you'll find it really difficult to deny yourself anything you fancy, whether it's a whole new outfit or a box of white Toblerones! Once you've got hold of whatever luxury goods you wanted you'll hang on to them like crazy — Rats are hoarders and hate to throw anything away!

Female Rats are almost always busy, they're good entertainers, which is just as well 'cos they have a really wide circle of friends, and when they fall in love they go all soppy, romantic and sentimental.

THE OX

All those born under the sign of the Ox are hard working and conscientious. They have their plan of action all worked out before they start anything so most things they do are methodical and practical. If you're an Ox you'll be a bit of a leader and you'll probably find that your pals will look to you to set the pace, they'll also admire you for your tough nature and unwillingness to compromise on matters you think are important.

Although Oxen trust and get on with people on the whole they tend to be loners who keep a fierce guard on their privacy and keep their deepest feelings to themselves. The Ox cherishes her independence and can be stubborn and obstinate and this can sometimes lead the Ox into problems with others. In these cases the Ox will usually use that famous stubbornness to stand firm and eventually get her own way but if, for some strange reason, she should lose she'll take defeat v. badly.

The Ox is also a great stickler for punctuality — she'll always be on time and nothing bugs her more than being kept waiting, especially if it's because of the other person's inefficiency. Due to her dependable nature the Ox usually does well in most jobs but she'll do best in politics, agriculture or careers that need specialised training.

Where romance is concerned the Ox goes in for long courtships while she gets to know the other person really well but once she is sure she'll remain devoted to her loved one.

THE TIGER

Wherever the Tiger goes there will be an atmosphere of excitement and change. The Tiger is born under the sign of courage and if you're a Tiger you'll do everything with bags of energy and enthusiasm and you'll always come up with new ideas for interesting things to do. You'll be a highly innovative thinker and you love a challenge so much you'll throw caution to the wind whenever you fancy and go away off to do your own thing!

On the negative side, because you're so impulsive and restless, you'll also find that you lose interest in things quickly too, so although you start doing a lot of interesting things, you quite often lack the staying power to see them through.

Your life will be a series of ups and downs and because you always feel so unsettled you'll often pack up and move on without too many backward glances. People like to spend time with you because of your liveliness but you can easily get into arguments through speaking your mind whether the situation demands it or not!

You'll probably marry when still quite young but you'll have problems in finding a suitable partner — not too many boys can stand the pace you live your life at and they often find your larger-than-life personality hard to deal with. It's their loss, though, because underneath your brash exterior you really are quite a sensitive soul!

THE CAT

In the East the Cat is regarded with a considerable amount of suspicion and mistrust but as you were born in the Year of the Cat you'll be refined, well-mannered and intelligent. You'll prefer a quiet, peaceful life and if you see any trouble brewing up on the horizon you'll do your best to keep well out of it!

Cats have a wide range of interests and they're particularly drawn to elegance and style. The Cat likes every aspect of her life to have style and she takes great care over her appearance. She places a lot of importance on her relationships with others, particularly those of the opposite sex. She will always have a lot of admirers and is quite likely to have a few serious relationships before settling down.

The Cat likes being with good friends, especially if there's a good discussion on the go, and her views will often be sought on a whole range of matters but the Cat will rarely lose her temper and chooses to let things other people say pass, even if they worry her. Loath to criticise others, the Cat also takes criticism v. badly.

Mystery and reserve are very much part of the Cat's character and she'll have an air of calm that some boys find really appealing — even when they are upset, Cats will always maintain their dignity!

THE DRAGON

If you're a Dragon the most remarkable thing about you is your luck! The Dragon is born under the sign of luck and loads of things fall into place for her without too much effort. You'll be a proud, intelligent and self-confident person who's a bit of an opportunist, always on the look out for a situation to take advantage of. You're intelligent and something of a perfectionist who always tries to do well at everything you take on.

The Dragon is outgoing and loves attracting publicity and attention. Dragons are at their best when they've got an audience to bring out the showman in them. If you're a Dragon you'll do well in showbusiness, where you'll be in the limelight, politics, or as a manager or boss of your own business.

You're sometimes too trusting, almost to the point of being gullible and if you feel as though you've been crossed you react in a sulky manner and it'll take you ages to either forgive or forget. Another bad point is your tendency to be over-confident which can lead you to make bad decisions. This is compounded by the fact that you're not too keen on taking anyone else's advice and you cherish your independence to such an extent that you'll probably remain single for a long time before you even consider letting anyone else in on your lifestyle. Oddly enough, because of your flamboyant personality and attractive physical appeal, you'll always have plenty admirers to choose from.

THE SNAKE

Mmmm, as a Snake you're a bit of a slippery character who has a very intelligent mind that's *always* thinking about something! Although you think deeply and like to meditate on things, you're also able to shed a few of your slippery skins and take on new places, people and jobs with enviable ease.

You're a good organiser especially where money is concerned and you'll always be quite well off as long as you resist the temptation to go to the local bingo house or back the odd horse in the Grand National — Snakes have the rare 'honour' of being the *worst* gamblers in the whole Chinese zodiac!

Although you use your intelligence to further your own ends you can easily hit health problems through burning up too much nervous energy. You'll do well in teaching, personnel and anything that involves research and planning.

Female snakes are incredibly stylish and graceful and they have great — and expensive — taste in clothes. You don't just splash out on yourself, though, you also really enjoy buying extravagant and luxurious presents for all your pals.

Amongst your bad points are your ruthlessness which sets people against you and your evasiveness that prevents you from really opening up to people and learning to trust them.

Love affairs are vital to the Snake and you'll probably have quite a few romances in your time although you always have to be given a measure of freedom or you'll quickly feel trapped.

THE HORSE

Elegance, charm and honesty are the chief characteristics of the Horse. You're naturally lively and sociable and people like you for your leadership qualities and your agile and able mind. Talking and debating are also your strong points.

You like nothing better than being the centre of attention and getting the chance to sound off about all your own thoughts and opinions.

You're independent and interested in a wide range of different activities although sometimes your interest is only superficial and you waste a lot of time and energy getting side-tracked in fads that are pretty meaningless. For all your independence you can be a little on the insecure side and you need lots of support and encouragement to make the most of yourself. Travel and exploring new places are very important to the Horse and you'll be tempted to live abroad at various times in your life.

For all your charm and elegance you have a not-very-stylish fiery temper which although short-lived you regret losing for some time after. Horses, perhaps due to their honesty, are also bad at keeping secrets.

The Horse spends a lot of time on her appearance and you're usually a rather unusual and distinctive dresser who's attractive to the opposite sex but who prefers to keep a little in reserve rather than getting totally wound up with their loved one.

THE GOAT

Goats are born under the sign of art so they are imaginative, creative and enjoy the finer things in life. You've got a calm easy-going nature and you like to spend a lot of time just enjoying yourself.

Self-discipline isn't one of your strong points so you prefer to work in a team rather than on your own when you're prone to get worried and unhappy. Given the chance, the Goat will let others make big decisions while she slopes off to get on with something that interests her more.

You are a follower rather than a leader, and because you crave security, you often go for relationships with older men.

The Goat is a very feminine sign and even most males born in the Year of the Goat show a strong feminine side.

Of all the signs in the Chinese zodiac the Goat is the most artistic and you like nothing better than getting on with creating something of artistic value. You're dreamy and changeable but if you feel really strongly about something you will defend your position to the last. You have a persuasive nature and know how to get your own way but you're always careful to keep your true feelings hidden, even though you'd get on much better if you were more forthright.

Where romance is concerned you like to live in a stable and secure environment and you'll be best suited to one of the more stable signs like the Pig or Cat.

THE MONKEY

Although in our society monkeys are thought of as being cheeky and mischievous, in Eastern cultures they are treated with much more respect. In the Chinese calendar the Monkey is born under the sign of fantasy and you're thought of as intelligent, quick-witted, imaginative and inquisitive. You like to keep an eye on everything that's going on around you!

You'll also be intelligent and well-read with a self-assured manner that can be very persuasive — you'll have little trouble in winning others around to your way of thinking and career-wise, you'd make a really good saleswoman. One of the Monkey's cleverest tricks is to build up other people's egos and make them think they're much more important that they really are — especially in the Monkey's eyes!

Fortunately for you, people don't realise that under your friendly, playful exterior you are actually a bit of a snob and you frequently look down your nose at others in a nasty manner.

You're an original thinker but you get bored easily and this could stop you from doing as well as you ought in your chosen career. It could also lead to problems in your love life, you're probably more interested in chasing around after boys you don't know too well rather than building up a steady relationship with a regular boyfriend. Failure doesn't seem to bother you too much, though, your usual reaction is just to shrug your shoulders and walk away.

THE ROOSTER

You have a truly flamboyant and colourful personality and you like nothing better than strutting around and showing off your fine feathers, especially in front of boys! You're dignified and have an air of authority but people sometimes get fed up with you if they feel you're a bit too full of yourself. You're always struggling to get in the limelight and this accounts for your loud manner and eye-catching clothes. It's not surprising that so many Roosters become actresses or dancers!

Being a little on the volatile side, you should try to restrain yourself a bit and not act on impulse which you'll almost always regret. Similarly, although you're a persuasive and interesting speaker, you do lack tact and it's all too easy for you to open your big mouth and cause a lot of trouble for yourself and other people!

The Rooster is usually a good organiser who likes to plan all her activities well in advance. If you're a Rooster you'll often carry around a notebook to jot down little reminders of what you should be doing and when — definitely a prime candidate for a Filofax! You're ambitious too but sometimes you make plans that are totally unrealistic and because you don't take criticism too well you won't listen if anybody tries to put you right.

In love you are very sincere and tend to stick to one boy at a time. A Snake or a Dragon would make a good partner but definitely swerve another Rooster — you'd just spend all your time squabbling.

THE DOG

True to all the old myths, people born in the Year of the Dog are incredibly loyal. You're not wimpy, though, you just hold your beliefs very strongly and you'll champion anything you think is a worthy cause. You're kind, too, and you'll always help out those less fortunate than yourself.

People never get the chance to take advantage of you because you're intuitively a good judge of character — you know what's what and don't let the side issues get in your way. You are quick and mentally alert and good to have around in a crisis 'cos you always keep your cool. Although you are friendly enough, you're not the world's greatest socialiser. Your idea of a fabby night out is a quiet meal with a few close friends.

You're not in the slightest bit materialistic and as long as you have money for yourself and friends you're perfectly happy, which is probably a good thing because whenever you do get hold of some dosh you tend to spend it like water!

In your career you'll probably do well in a job where you can help others, perhaps medicine or law, but be careful to keep yourself motivated or else you could just drift through life without ever achieving anything.

Fortunately, despite your changeable moods, you're never too short of potential boyfriends who respond to your warm and caring nature. Avoid Goats and Roosters at all costs — they'll only get on your nerves!

THE PIG

You're honest, kind and understanding and wherever possible, you try to keep the peace and sort out unpleasantness. You like to get straight to the point, speak truthfully and avoid anything that even smacks of hypocrisy. You're willing to put a lot of effort into everything you do, whether it's joining a club, where you'll be a good committee member or fundraiser, or in the way you relate to other people. You love to amuse others and you have a great sense of humour.

Giving up your own time to help others is never a problem to you but sometimes you'd be well-advised to stand firm and not be cajoled into something you don't really want to do. Nothing will get you down for too long, though, you have a strong character and bounce back from bad times relatively quickly. Although you tend to spend your money quite freely you are also astute in financial matters and there are loads of Pigs who have become v. wealthy. They often make successful businessmen, particularly if they've had to fight their way back from some run of bad luck.

Dearest to the Pig's heart is a great love of food and drink, you're a real pleasure seeker and think nothing of spending all your hard-earned cash on a fancy slap-up meal.

Provided you don't let anyone take advantage of your good nature and you learn to assert yourself a little more, you'll have a happy life and you'll be able to establish a good relationship with most boys you meet — with the exception of the Snake!

SKI TIPS

If you're a sucker for the ski-slopes then make sure you don't let your skin suffer.

Use a good ski cream to protect your skin from the damaging rays of the sun and the harsh weather conditions. A protective lip salve is a must too, to keep your lips soft.

Before you head for the slopes, it's a good idea to do a few exercises to help prevent muscle aches and pains.

Start slowly, gradually building up to a regular exercise session.

Warm up with some stretching exercises first then try a few of these routines . . .

● Stand straight, feet together, arms relaxed. Bend the right knee, lifting the leg up to waist height, and repeat six times. Now do the same, bringing your knee up diagonally across. Change to left leg and repeat.

● Lie on the floor on your back and gradually sit up, keeping your feet on the floor. Repeat six times.

● Kneel on the floor, knees slightly apart, feet together. Hold arms out in front and, keeping your body straight, slowly lean back as far as you can then slowly return to the upright position. Repeat four times.

Always cool down after exercising by relaxing your body and shaking out your arms and legs.

TOP TEN CHRISTMAS SONGS
1. White Christmas — Bing Crosby
2. Do They Know It's Christmas? — Band Aid
3. Party Party — Elvis Costello
4. Merry Christmas Everybody — Slade
5. Jingle Bells — Santa Claus(!)
6. I Wish It Could Be Christmas Every Day — Wizzard
7. Happy Christmas War Is Over — John Lennon
8. Mary's Boy Child — Boney M
9. It's My Party — Dave Stewart with Barbara Gaskin
10. Last Christmas — Wham!

WHAT THIS SEASON HAS IN STORE.
WAKE UP TO

PROMISES! PROMISES!

How to keep those New Year Resolutions . . .

I resolve to stop biting my nails

This can be a tough one but with a lot of willpower and some extra-strong nail products you *can* do it! First of all, get your nails into shape with an emery board. Always file from the side to the centre — not in a see-saw fashion as this will encourage the nails to break. Apply a clear nail hardener to your nails and keep telling yourself how nice they look! If you can't resist the urge to nibble then reach for a carrot instead! Once they've reached a reasonable length apply a pale coloured varnish with a clear top coat for extra protection. You'll be so proud of your pretty, coloured nails you won't even be tempted to nibble — will you?!

I resolve to pass my exams

This needn't be as hard as it sounds if you work out a proper revision schedule beforehand. Even if you're an avid EastEnders fan you'll still be able to fit in a bit of swotting and if you do this regularly then you won't have to miss any episodes of your favourite soap at exam time. To make the most of your study time shut yourself in your bedroom away from the telly and copies of Jackie. To make things a bit more interesting, why not try recording some questions on a tape recorder leaving a short gap where you'll hopefully be able to think of the answers, then give the actual answer. With practice you should soon know it off by heart!

PARTY! PARTY!

Parties are a brilliant excuse for going a bit over the top . . .

● Go for some glitter — in your hair or on your body. Check out Christmas make-up kits for some sparkly shades.

● Treat yourself to a 'little black number' and jazz it up with bright accessories and fancy tights or stockings.

● Be bold with your make-up and go for bright red lipstick for the perfect pout under the mistletoe.

BIG SOFTIES!

Moisturising is one of the most important words for winter as far as your skin is concerned. Wind, rain, snow and central-heating can all dry up your skin, making it taut and flaky.

Combat the winter weather by taking extra-special care of your skin. Invest in a good hand cream, body lotion and light moisturiser for your face and neck.

Don't neglect your lips either — a good lip salve worn alone or over lipstick will make all the difference.

JACKIE XM

By William A

C A

Cind
Ugly Sist
Fairy Godfat
Prince Charm
Butt
Gi
Dick Whitting
Dick Whittington's
J
Beanst
Direc
Produ
Best
Key G

Cinders

Ugly Sisters

AS PANTO

even Shakespeare

Fairy Godfather

ACT 1

Storm clouds scudded across the face of the full moon. A lone wolf howled, the bitter wind whipped bitterly through the leafless trees surrounding the Dark Satanic Castle. EastEnders was just finishing . . .

Inside the d.s.c. (dark satanic castle) a peroxide blonde, no wait brunette, slip of a girl is screaming abuse at a hoover.

Cinders — Bloomin' thing! It never works! I'm fed up cleaning this castle anyway. It takes too long. How am I supposed to get to the disco!

(At this point Cinderella's two rather ugly sisters enter the room.)

Tall Ugly Sister — You won't get to the disco in time to meet any nice young men! Isn't that right, sister!

Grumpy, Small Sister — Hmph! S'pose so!

Tall Ugly Sister — Well we can't stop here chattering to you, you little wretch! We're going to get ready for tonight's disco, eh, sister?

Grumpy, Small Sister — Hmph! S'pose so!

(The uggos flounce out leaving Cinders fiddling with the hoover, a screwdriver and some fuse wire. Suddenly she leaps to her feet and starts having a tantrum.)

Cinders — S'not fair! I bet there'll be loads of talent at the disco. But I can't go because those two horrors won't give me the bus fare! Nobody cares about me!

(RASPPPP!! Sound effect. And nothing happens. Cinderella notices a portly bloke trying to squeeze through the window.)

Fairy Godfather — *(for 'tis he)* — Come on, Cinders! Give me a hand! I'm stuck!

(Cinders pulls tubby bloke in a tutu in through the window. He waves a crumpled bent wand.)

Buttons

Fairy Godfather — I'm your Fairy Godfather, sweetie. And I'm here to grant you three wishes!

Cinders — Why not grant yourself a hit single then! Giggle!

Fairy Godfather — I'll ignore that remark, you minx. Er — I mean, you shall go to the ball, em, disco.

Cinders — Ace! I'll get me gear on!

(Fairy Godfather produces sickeningly sweet and nice party frock.)

Fairy Godfather — I've got a super little party number for you here, dear.

(Cinders reappears in black basque with tassles, fishnets and stilettos.)

Cinders — I'm not wearing that thing. Give it to Pepsi and Shirlie! This is my boogie gear!

Fairy Godfather — Yes, well, em, now for the question of how to get to the ball, erm, disco! Have you got a pumpkin?

(Cinders rummages about in vegetable rack, produces turnip.)

Cinders — Will this do?

Fairy Godfather — Ahem! Not what I'm used to working with but I'll see what I can do . . .

(He waves his wand daintily and there's a thunderous crash and the Top Of The Pops theme music plays distantly . . . the smoke clears to reveal a gleaming limousine where the turnip had been. Unfortunately it's broken most of the furniture in the room.)

Fairy Godfather — *(dead chuffed with himself)* — . . . hmm, still got the old magic touch I see!

Cinders — Yeyhah! Let's go! I'll drive!

Fairy Godfather — You will not! I've got a driver for you!

(Waves the wand with a little more confidence this time . . . thunderous crash, smoke, etc . . . When all the action's over they're confronted by a cheeky looking boy with a lovely smile!)

Fairy Godfather — Meet Buttons, Cinders! He's your driver!

Cinders — Fwoah!

Fairy Godfather — Come back, I haven't told you what time to get home!

(They zoom off in limo. They haven't gone very far when they feel a bump.)

Cinders — What was that bump?

Buttons — Your heart, doll?

(Bruised figure slowly detaches himself from the tarmac and groans.)

Dick Whittington — Moan! Who wants to go to London anyway?

Dick Whittington's cat — You do, you wally!

(Limo comes to an impressive skidding halt outside posh disco. There is a huge great beanstalk growing outside the disco entrance.)

Buttons *(to Cinders)* — Fancy nipping into that bush for a snog, duchess?

(At this a very small boy appears.)

Giant — That's not a bush! It's a 450 ft. beanstalk!

Buttons — And who might you be, mush?

Giant *(proudly)* — I'm The Giant!

Gia

90

All — Haw-haw-haw! Bit small aren't you?

Giant — Shurrup! I'm little for my size!

(Cinders heads into the disco, leaving Buttons watching the limo.)

INTERMISSION

(Readers are requested to hurry up in the loos and to raid the fridge quickly because the panto re-starts in the next paragraph.)

ACT 2

(Cinders stands sipping a Coke watching the dance floor and looking bored. She sees her ugly sisters swanking about and sticks her tongue out at them.)

Cinders — What a dead loss this is!

Voice — Do you come here often?

Cinders *(turns)* — What's it got to do with . . . bloomin 'eck!

(Cinders almost swoons as she's confronted by the most gorgeous boy she's ever seen.)

Prince Charming — Quite a jolly do, eh?

Cinders — Sure! Wanna dance?

(A dozen boogies later Cinders finally drags an exhausted Prince Charming off the floor.)

Cinders — I've got to go now! Look at the time!

Prince Charming — Why? Will you turn into a turnip?

Cinders — No, the chip shop shuts soon!

(She runs away, leaving one Doc Marten shoe behind. Prince Charming picks it up, sniffs it and falls down in a faint!)

Cinders — Buttons! Joe's Chippie now!

Buttons — Yes, mam!

(He slams the limo into reverse and bashes into the beanstalk. It topples and they zoom off, leaving behind a tearful small Giant.)

Giant — I am a giant! I am! I am!

(Two bruised and battered figures emerge from under a beanstalk watched by a cat.)

Dick Whittington — Groan! Who are you?

Prince Charming

Jack — I'm Jack and that was my bloomin' beanstalk!

Dick Whittington — Let's take it to my place in London and have it on toast!

Dick Whittington's Cat — What nerds!

ACT 3

(Cinders in her house, reading Jackie while the Ugly Sisters vainly plaster themselves with make-up. There's a knock at the door and Prince Charming walks in, with a clothes peg on his nose and holding a Doc Marten shoe.

Prince Charming — I want to know whose shoe this is!

Tall Ugly Sister — Mine, actually!

(She slips it on and unfortunately it fits. Prince Charming and Cinders look horror-struck.

Tall Ugly Sister — See! It fits me!

Prince Charming and Cinders — Run for it!

(They exit stage left chased by a tall ugly sister.)

ACT 4

(RASPPPP! The Fairy Godfather re-appears with even more crumpled and bent wand.)

Fairy Godfather — This thing's got one wish left in it — I'll give it to you lot out there! May you never have to read such a lot of old tosh ever again!

(Thunderous crash, smoke . . .)

THE END